WORSHIP 2000

RESOURCES TO CELEBRATE
THE NEW MILLENNIUM

Reasons and resources
for celebrating the beginning of a new millennium,
with messages for the new millennium
from twenty Christian leaders and scholars
from around the world

PETER ATKINS

D1426026

Fount
An Imprint of HarperCollins*Publishers*

Fount is an Imprint of
HarperCollins*Publishers*
77–85 Fulham Palace Road, London W6 8JB

First published in Great Britain in 1999 by
HarperCollinsPublishers
1 3 5 7 9 10 8 6 4 2

A catalogue record for this book
is available from the British Library.

ISBN 0 00 599377 6

Printed and bound in Great Britain by
Creative Print and Design (Wales), Ebbw Vale

CONTENTS

PREFACE

This book would not have been written without the encouragement of so many people, particularly my wife Rosemary and my daughter Susan. They so often cheer me on, convincing me that I have something useful to say, during the periods when I doubt that there is anyone who is interested in listening. Together as a family we have learned to celebrate, even when there are difficulties all around us. It is in this spirit of celebration and thankfulness that we should all rejoice as the new millennium begins.

This book was also inspired by my visits during 1996 to some places of worship worldwide where the Spirit of God is very evident and the energy and excellence of the worship is part of a loving, humble, human response to that Spirit. My understanding of worship and culture, of the global nature of our one world and of the revelation of God in Jesus Christ was enhanced by these visits.

In Chapter 6 of this book I have expressed my thanks to a wide range of people who have joined me in this enterprise. I was thrilled to have the input of younger people to help draft some of the prayers; of some of the most senior figures in the worldwide Christian community to add their messages of guidance as we begin the new millennium; of Christian scholars who have pointed out issues of deep significance as we ponder the meaning of the year AD 2000; and of a small group of representative musicians who generously shared their talents with us, suggesting the words and music we might sing at worship occasions during the year. The responsibility for the selection and the texts rests solely with me, but without the help of so many others this book would not have the richness that this significant celebration deserves.

I am grateful to James Catford and to Kathy Dyke of HarperCollins*Religious* in London for their input as experienced publishers and editors in bringing the project to fruition, and for their personal guidance and patience over the rather long period of settling on the best way to present the material.

As the final manuscript for this book was being put together the passing of the years was noted in a defining way with the death of the recently retired Archbishop of the Church in Aotearoa, New Zealand and Polynesia. Brian Davis had been a friend and companion of mine since 1960, when I first arrived in New Zealand. We were priests together, we played squash together, we had served parishes and dioceses together, we had affirmed faith together, and our two families have shared much of life's joys and trials together. Brian was a skilled carver, water-colour artist, social commentator, author, preacher, leader and organizer. He listened well and he spoke well in the name of God. With the publication of this book I honour him.

The pilgrimage into the new millennium will not be the same without him, but our faith in resurrection will be even firmer, and we will still celebrate the year 2000 together – for the past, the present and the future are all in God's hands, and to God be the glory at all times. This book is my invitation to you, the reader, to echo the opening words of Michael Baughen's hymn, and 'Come celebrate' this new millennium – God's time and ours.

INTRODUCTION

For me it all began at Nazareth in Galilee. No, I was not born there, but the seed of this book was planted there in 1996 when I visited the Church of the Annunciation. Built above an ancient cave in Jesus' home town, this Christian basilica is a parable of our worship today as the millennium turns another circle.

From the outside the church looks modern, built like a corona as a sign of honour to the Queen of Heaven, Mary the mother of Jesus the Christ, who was born into the family of Joseph and Mary some time about 2000 years ago. Inside the church the ancient cave, where early tradition says that Mary heard God's message of new birth, lies deep in an undercroft. The space above it has been left open so that it is like a circle in the floor at each of the subsequent levels. Beside the cave is a chapel with its own altar where the pilgrims of today gather to give thanks for this great event in the history of mankind. Above is a vast basilica whose walls are decorated with the art of the cultures of the modern world. They depict the Christ and his Mother with the features and clothes of many nations. Then in the apse of the church there is the high altar whose ceiling-dome pictures the Christ reigning in glory, surrounded by the saints of every age, with Mary his Mother crowned in radiance in a central place.

This symbolism in art and architecture is a true sign of the reality of worship and faith among Christians today. For them the seed planted at this spot has spread its branches to every corner of the earth, where it has taken root in every culture and generation. So the Mother and Child can be truly painted in the clothes and features of Mexico, Japan, Ireland, Africa, Italy, Poland, America, Germany and more besides.

The year 2000 will be marked by the governments of the world as an occasion to present new plans for a new millennium. These governments will look forward, making hopeful promises for the future, rather than taking a balanced view and also looking backwards to acknowledge the muddles as well as the achievements of humanity. Technology will be displayed as providing the miracles for this future, and the governments of the powerful nations will point their peoples to the heavens as their space-craft lift off into the skies.

However, at the turn of the millennium individuals are likely to be more cautious about dreaming of a new tomorrow. In our throw-away society, where change is rapid and turnover speedy, people are weary from the struggle to survive day by day in a world which has lost its power to give value to each individual.

Confused by history and change, Christians may hesitate to point out to others that the date of the year 2000 can only be significant if the Incarnation of God in Christ is taken seriously. After all, the 'AD' in 'AD 2000' stands for *Anno Domini*, 'in the year of our Lord', despite the modern fashion to be respectful of other religions and refer to 2000 CE, where 'CE' means 'Common Era'. Despite this concession, the other major religions seem to retain their own systems of dating. Jews refer to Jerusalem 3000, and among the Chinese people it will be 'the year of the Dragon'. For Christians to witness to their faith at the time of the celebrations of the year 2000 they will need to regain their confidence in the importance for history of Jesus, the Christ, conceived at Nazareth and reborn in the hearts of his followers in every generation and culture.

The purpose of this book is to help Christians revive that confidence and celebrate the year 2000 with worship that is true to its roots and yet imbedded in their own culture and generation. Christians believe that Jesus was both truly human and truly divine and thus affirms for us the principle of both/and rather than that of either/or. In the same way, the worship of that Christ brings together both our current culture and gener-ation and our roots in the time, place and culture which the Son of God entered 2000 years ago.

Christians will in part find this confidence by looking back to the begin-ning of the current millennium for inspiration. That new millennium gave birth to the flowering of a major period of Christian witness. In his concise overview of the course of Christian times, *A History of Christianity*, Kenneth Latourette of Yale University writes: 'Not far from the year 950 a fresh surge of life was seen in Christianity which was to continue until about the year 1350.'[1] Many of the peoples of Northern Europe will be celebrating the one thousandth anniversary of the emergence of the Christian faith in their lands. At the beginning of this millennium Greek Christianity spread rapidly in Russia, building on earlier advances. In the eleventh century Norse Christianity reached Greenland, and probably the shores of North America. In those years Christianity even spread again to form pockets of believers in India and China.

At the start of that new millennium a new energy of Christianity and of trade prosperity was born. The monastic movement gave new power to personal devotion and liturgy. The 'Mother House' at Cluny spread its revival of discipline and faith to its many daughter houses throughout Europe. Soon Bernard of Clairvaux was deepening the devotion of many believers. Then the Friars took the message out to the rich and poor of the new towns, and Francis of Assisi combined practical Christianity with obedience and simplicity.

For such a new burst of energy to happen again, Christians will need to be ready to give answers to a series of questions which have rarely been clearly answered during the last century. This has been a time when there were so many conflicting voices that Christians became confused. Christians will also need to express their thoughts in a way that makes sense to ordinary people. This book will attempt to provide pointers for the responses to the queries we face, so that we can all find our own words to answer such questions as these:

In the year 2000 ...
- Is it possible for us to celebrate our history as Christians when there is so much debate by Christians about the historical basis of our faith?
- Do we want to mark Jesus' beginnings at Nazareth and Bethlehem, when these places are the subject of so much tension between the Jewish and Palestinian peoples?
- What does it mean to say that Jesus became 'one of us' at the Incarnation, now that humanity is so diverse and different from his generation?
- Is there a unity in being human which is greater than the diversity of race, gender and age?
- Can Christ, who intercedes for us, understand the experiences behind our prayers, now that life is so different from the days when he was on earth?

- Can we still bear public witness to Christ in worship, when we live in a multi-faith and pluralistic world?
- Would it help us if we were to visit Nazareth, in the hope that we would find Jesus more real there than at our local place of worship?
- In a multi-media age, how can we use liturgical art and drama to connect the Jesus of history with the Christ of worship?
- How can we avoid each Christian denomination competing with its neighbour and instead plan for a unified Christian celebration of the new millennium?
- Can we link traditional with contemporary modes of worship so that we have resources for personal and corporate use to celebrate 'Worship 2000'?

In Part 1 of this book (Chapters 1–5) I attempt to address the first nine questions. In Part 2 (Chapters 6–11) I offer resources for our personal and corporate worship, as a response to the last question in the list.

In Chapter 1, 'Confident Christians', I examine whether Christians can talk of Christianity as an 'historical religion'. I am convinced that the Christ of the Incarnation is the very bedrock of our Christian faith. Our current experience witnesses to the truth that the risen and ascended Lord is able to relate to us in our time and place. Yet this contemporary experience must remain attached to the roots of the historical Jesus, so that we avoid the temptation to shape Christ in our own likeness. The Jesus of history and the Christ of faith must always remain linked. This is another example of the both/and principle, and Christians must not succumb to the false doctrine of the either/or of materialistic definitions.

One of the elements in the recovery of confidence in our historical faith is the evidence of archaeology, and the perspective it gives us of time and place. In Chapter 2, 'Our Roots at Nazareth', I will take you on a word pilgrimage to the sites of Nazareth and Bethlehem to inspire us to recapture our roots and see them as a vital part of our inheritance. The current struggle of the peoples who inhabit that land should help us to work for peace and reconciliation – the *shalom* of God – as part of our mission and our prayers as we begin the new millennium.

Such prayers will lead us into Chapter 3, 'Holding Hands at Prayer', as we consider what prayer means for a Christian and how we are linked in our humanity with one another and with Christ, despite the differences between generations, genders and cultures. We now often stress such differences, hoping thereby to show greater respect for those who differ from us. By doing this we can overlook the much greater proportion of our thinking and being that we share with one another in our common humanity. Some words of Archbishop Desmond Tutu helped me to see this truth:

> This Jesus Christ, whatever we may have done, has broken down all that separates us irrelevantly – such as race, sex, culture, status, etc. In this Jesus Christ we are for ever bound together as one redeemed humanity, black and white together.[2]

Desmond Tutu has worked hard by his actions and his prayers to bring about reconciliation and justice in his continent. He can be a model for us all as we move into the new millennium. It is a time when all the peoples of the world will need to learn to live together as one Rainbow People of God.

In Chapter 4, 'Holding Hands across the Globe', I encourage all Christians to take their place as part of the 'great multitude that no one can count, from every nation, from all tribes and peoples and languages',[3] and to span the continents in the praise and worship of God. The occasion of 'Worship 2000' can draw us together and allow us to share in the various cultures of global Christianity.

We can draw on the rhythm of the worship of Africa, on the reflective musical worship of Britain, on the value of silence in worship from Taizé in France, on the mystic worship of Eastern Christianity, on the magnitude of worship in the Americas, on the worship of the Creator God of the Pacific, and on the contemplative and compassionate worship of India. Yet we know it is the one Holy Spirit which enables this diversity of gifts for the building up of the one Body of Christ.[4]

The television producers will relay the pictures of the dawn of the year 2000 into our homes and capture the globe in a single piece. We too can make the world our village and feel at home with our neighbours in all their diversity. In this chapter my aim is to bring your neighbour's worship into your mind's eye so that you can feel its spirit and thereby enliven your local worship as the new millennium dawns.

Chapter 5, 'Worship for a New Millennium', is the final chapter in Part 1 of the book. In it I will suggest some new directions that we might take for contemporary worship. Writing as I do from 'Down Under', it is best for me to set out some principles with examples, and allow each reader or congregation to put them into practice for themselves in a way that accords with their own culture and generation. Worship must be rooted in the realities of a time and place, as well as in the continuing Gospel.

The principle of the Incarnation is still at work in worship as it was at Nazareth in the presence of God in the humanity of Mary and Jesus.

Part 2 of this book provides some resources for the celebration of 'Worship 2000'. Worship is always both corporate and personal, so I have tried to provide resources for both these settings. The year 2000 gives Christians opportunities to cooperate to achieve one major joint celebration to witness to their faith and involve the whole community in which they are placed. It also gives an opportunity for local congregations and individuals to focus on this theme in a more regular way throughout the year in their own setting. I have attended to the needs of each in turn.

In Chapter 7 I set forth some 'Outlines of Services for Public Worship'. The two major Christian festivals which are the most suitable for the community as a whole to mark the beginning of the new millennium are the Feast of the Epiphany and the Feast of the Ascension. The first festival highlights the revelation of Christ to the world, and the second focuses on the drawing of all humanity into the heart of God. The weather in the two hemispheres may determine which is the most suitable choice between these two dates. If early summer is the best time for a large community gathering, then Christians in the southern hemisphere may choose to celebrate 'Worship 2000' with a public service on the Feast of the Epiphany on 6 January. Such a date in the northern hemisphere may be impossible in the snows of mid-winter. Christians there may choose early summer as the most suitable time, and celebrate the Feast of the Ascension on 1 June with worship to mark the new millennium. In addition to these Festivals, Professor Stookey in Washington DC suggested to me that the turn of the year was a suitable time for a community celebration. I have therefore included an outline of an inter-faith service entitled 'Into the future'. Chapter 7 provides outline services for each of these occasions and gives responsibility to local people to fill in the outlines according to their situation.

In Chapter 8, 'Themes, Readings and Prayers for Congregational Worship', I have gathered material which I believe is suitable for congregational worship any time during the year 2000. I have chosen seven themes which arise out of the material in Chapters 1–5. The readings provide passages of Scripture relating to these themes, giving the Bible reference and a brief title to each passage. These passages speak of the way that Christians should worship and serve if they are to obey Micah's call to 'walk humbly with your God'.[5] The prayers include a small number of 'collects' which could be used regularly within a congregation during the year. The collects are followed by a selection of prayers on each of the themes. These prayers were composed with the help of young people in

New Zealand. Chapter 8 ends with an 'Intercession of thanksgiving and hope for a new millennium'.

In Chapter 9, 'Prayers and Reflections for Personal Worship', I have written and collected some prayers which are more suitable for personal use. These prayers allow for times of reflection and intercession. The Christian faith has always touched our personal as well as our corporate life. It encourages us to develop the spirit within us as well as the spirit between us. I hope that these prayers might prove useful for that inner journey, and be a springboard for adoration and enhance our appreciation of the work of God in our own lives.

In Chapter 9 I have included prayers which help us to enter into a dialogue with God about our relationship with God, and God's care for us. I trust that these prayers, based on the compositions of younger people, can be used as vehicles to bring us into the presence of God; there to be transformed in heart and mind, so that we practise in our lives what we have discovered in reflective prayer.

The final group of prayers in Chapter 9 is under the title 'Life in the new millennium' and includes the hopes and dreams of the young for life inspired by a caring and just God.

I was fortunate to have friends and contacts throughout the world to enable me to gather in Chapter 10 a collection of 'Messages for a new millennium' from 20 representative Christian leaders and scholars. Their messages bring hope and challenge to us as we face the first years of a new century, and provide a perspective of Christian activity and vision from the various regions of the world. Read together as a whole, they will inspire us to be faithful and thoughtful as we reflect on God's message for us today. I hope that congregations and individuals will use the messages as spring-boards for their own determination to use the Spirit's power for Christian witness and action in their local communities.

In Chapter 11, 'Hymns and Songs for a New Millennium', I have gathered from a number of sources hymns and songs from my own culture in the hope that it might inspire those from other cultures to also honour this occasion with new words and tunes. We need to be able to express to God our hopes and dreams, our words of praise and thanksgiving, our pleas for comfort and care, in tune with the culture and form of each generation. A new dawn calls for new songs, and I hope that others may follow the example of those who have so kindly contributed to this collection. The copyright for the words and music is retained by the authors or their agents, and I am grateful to them for permission to include the works in this book.

In the Conclusion I have put forward one final word of encouragement for all Christians to seize the opportunity of the beginning of the new millennium to give witness to their faith and to worship their God in an event or a series of events which might be called 'Worship 2000'.

My prayer is that this book will stir you into action and provide you with resources that will enable your worship. Let this be done to the glory of God and give rise to the spread of the Good News of our Saviour Jesus Christ as the new millennium begins.

1

CONFIDENT CHRISTIANS

Christians have suffered a crisis of confidence in the last 100 years. Their intellectual integrity has been under attack from pseudo-scientific quarters that wished to claim that everything which was non-material or not able to be externally 'proved' was non-existent. Their emotional integrity has been under attack from those who claimed that religion was a prop for immature human beings. Their moral integrity has been under attack from those who believed that all moral teaching was oppressive and thus restricted individual freedom. Their historical integrity has been under attack from those who claimed that there was no historical proof for the dates and the people contained in the scriptural records. Their world-view was under attack in the light of space exploration and geological research. Their evangelistic zeal was resisted by those who considered all religion to hold equal truth and value.

Even within the Church, the ordinary follower of Christ found that their simple faith was under criticism from some of those who held positions of leadership in their Church. Therefore they often hid the faith that meant so much to them, fearing that if they revealed a faith based on their own experience others might declare it uncritical, unthinking or childlike. In defence many claimed 'to know what they believed', but they had no wish to share it with others for fear that it might not be acceptable to them. The Christian statements of faith, including the traditional Creeds, were no longer the declaration of confident Christians, but were said to be historical documents open to personal reinterpretation. From Harnack to Jenkins and then Spong, the writings of 'thinkers' left Christians with encouragement to do good works, but with little intellectual integrity. As a result the louder God was declared non-existent or even 'dead', the more life was sought from demonstrations of spiritual power. People gained reassurance from feeling the power and warmth of the Spirit rather than from knowledge arising out of thinking and research into Christian doctrine.

Now the turning of the century as well as the millennium is proving to be a turning point in attitudes for Christians. There is a movement towards bringing things together, reaching a consensus of respect for truth, working on the both/and principle rather than demanding that things are either this or that.

Now people are more ready to allow the use of specific languages for different types of knowledge. Computer users have their own language to articulate their particular concepts. Mathematics is regarded as having a language to convey the thoughts and ideas of that field of learning. Cultures have realized that they need to retain specific language to convey their own particular concepts and ideas, and that translation into the language of another culture may not convey the whole range of ideas associated with a particular cultural term. So the Christian religion is regaining its confidence to claim to have a 'language' for its experiences of God, Jesus Christ and the Holy Spirit, and to gently but firmly assert its right to use such language to convey truth, even in the face of those who want to claim that such language is meaningless. Such use of specific language demands that people first share knowledge and learning, and also enter into shared experiences and feelings. It demands that the enquirer and even the sceptic give time and effort to understand such language at depth before dismissing it as falling outside their own knowledge and experience.

This new attitude to ideas, language and culture also requires Christians to be learned and articulate. Christians now realize the need for the sort of communication which takes the listener and their needs as seriously as those of the speaker. Christians know that they cannot make themselves clear simply by repeating key phrases and long nouns. Such words as 'Son of God' and 'salvation' have to be unpacked and filled out with both knowledge and experience. The next 100 years may well be labelled by historians as 'the age of communication'. Communication (in contrast to propaganda) presupposes a relationship between sender and receiver, speaker and listener. Once we refer to relationship, we are incorporating ideas of respect, love, forgiveness, friendship, care and development. For Christians communication is at the heart of the Gospel – God's initiative in communication by word, and by the Word made flesh in Jesus Christ, and by the word as inspired by the Holy Spirit.

Christians find that they no longer need to be defensive in making such assertions, but only to ask for respect and time from others with whom they wish to communicate for the sake of discovering the truth. Younger people in this new century, brought up with greater diversity, a greater range of knowledge, a deeper respect for other cultures, are more ready to ask the spiritual questions that lead into two-way communication. For younger people, with their eyes to the future, the turn of the millennium is of greater interest, since their lives lie ahead of them in the age to come. As they do so, they also want to look back to the roots of things, because they know that the experience of the past is valuable, and in itself has shaped both the present and the future.

I am sure that Christians are in a key position to contribute to the shaping of this future. Their faith has always been built upon the deep roots of the past, on the initiatives of God in creation and in history, on living in the present as the 'now' of the actions of God in salvation and in inspiration, and on moving into the future as the goal of personal and corporate fulfilment. It is for this reason that the year 2000 gives Christians unique opportunities to communicate their faith and also contribute to the shaping of the new century and the new millennium. The year 2000 allows us to acknowledge the past – the initiative of the Incarnation and its turning point in the history of humanity – and to plan for the future, paying particular attention to the key issues of human relationships, the care of creation, peace and justice, and above all, the re-establishment of a sense of worth, value and humility in each person in the new global community.

With this reassurance that Christians are able to communicate with confidence with their neighbours, it is time to tackle the first of the questions which were posed in the Introduction: *Is it possible for us to celebrate our history as Christians, when there is so much debate among Christians about the historical basis of our faith?*

First, it can be said firmly that Christianity has always been an 'historical' religion – that is, one in which it is claimed that there were events in history which have shaped the relationship between God and humanity. Some religions do not see God as involved in the history of human existence. In their tenets God enters into a contemporary timeless relationship with the worshipper or devotee. Other religions are based on a relationship with the Divine that is inherent in the natural elements around us – river, tree, mountains and the like. Unlike these, Christianity claims that God has been active in an historical line of events, and is still active in the present as much as in the past. The future too is in God's hands until the end of time as we know it. History as well as personal experience is therefore the sphere of God's activity. From this view point the 'date' is a matter of important record, and that is why we have a year AD 2000 to celebrate. Time does not pass without significance but is a framework for events which have a connection and a purpose. Time starts somewhere and is going somewhere. It has a beginning, a past, a present and a future. For a Christian, God is active in each part of this continuum. Before time there was God; at this point of time there is God; at the end of time there will be God; and then there will be a new order of time and existence as gifted by God.

Christianity in this sense is an historical religion. To communicate this with clarity we also have to add that this statement does not mean that God's activity was more real in the past (in history) than it is in the present, or will be in the future. That is not the experience of Christians down the generations. Unfortunately, in the English language we often use the word 'remember' to mean 'look back into the past', and this gives rise to an impression that Christians have a nostalgic attitude to their faith when they use the word 'remember' in their worship. However, for the Christian the word 'remember' carries with it a Hebrew association of meaning which conveys the concept, 'to make the past present with power'. Thus to remember an event is to bring that event to mind so that it has the powerful significance that it had at the time when it first occurred. The Hebrew people remembered the Passover in Egypt as an event whose significance for their relationship with God was renewed each year at the Passover Festival. This attitude to the past has been incorporated into the meaning of the words used in worship during the Christian Festivals. The worship at every Christmas makes the significance of the Incarnation and birth of Jesus powerful again for those who participate in that worship. Every Good Friday the worshipper is in touch again with the power of the sacrificial death of Jesus Christ. Every Easter Christ is raised again from the tomb to make clear his victory over the grave and his conquest of all the enemies of life and goodness. These 'past' events are made present again through this remembrance, and their power is available to the faithful and to all those who will be in touch with these dramatic historical events. All these events are summed up in the remembrance during the Great Thanksgiving Prayer at Holy Communion.

Christianity is also historical in another way. Its records are open to archaeological and comparative literature research. In the last hundred years or so both these activities have been pursued with vigour and sometimes with arrogance. However, we now have sufficient material to establish a reasonable picture both of events and their contexts. The

modern state of Israel has been particularly active in meticulous archaeological research, and the treasures that lay buried under the surface of the
earth and the sea have been uncovered to give us a clearer picture of the
past. You will find some of the details of this work in the next chapter, but I
want to look at some of the principles now to establish Christian confidence and credibility.

The principles behind the archaeological research flow from such questions as these:

- What happened on this site at various times in the past?
- What record has been left of these happenings?
- What dates can be attached to these records?

Answering such questions helps to build up a picture of the context of the
lives of the people who lived in this place in their particular generation. We
can learn much about this context from the buildings that they erected,
from the layout of the community, from the artefacts they used, and from
the signs of industry and trade.

A visit to the site of Caesarea, the Roman garrison headquarters on the
Mediterranean coast of Israel just above the current city of Tel Aviv, helped
me to see how each of these signs contributed to the context with which to
read Christian literature of the first century AD. The size of the site is
impressive. It contains the outline foundation of numerous buildings,
some of which have been reconstructed. These include the garrison headquarters and a very large amphitheatre, with entrances for gladiators and
wild animals and a stage from which the sea breezes carry the voices so
that they can be heard in each part of the tiered seating. On the beach
there is preserved a long section of the elaborate aqueduct which carries
a small river to the site. There is a boat harbour and many community
buildings, indicating that this was a sizable settlement of Roman life. The
artefacts displayed there showed me that this was a sensitive, creative
society in which sculpture was true to life and the human form was treated
with respect. For me the most powerful item on display was a large stone
tablet on which were inscribed words commemorating an event 'in the
presence of Pontius Pilate the Governor'. Through this stone the past for
me vividly became a tangible event. I was in touch with history, the history
which was on my lips every time I recited the words 'under Pontius Pilate'
in the Church's Creeds. Pilate had stood here, representing locally all the
power and authority of an empire that stretched from the Tiber right
across the Mediterranean to this remote spot on a foreign shore. Such

context makes it clear that governors could order the crucifixion of those who crossed their path to cause rebellion. Peace and justice should go hand in hand, but if necessary justice could be sacrificed for the sake of the *Pax Romana*.

Yet this site also showed the other side of human nature – the love of art, the skill of engineer and craftsman, and the desire to live together in community. It revealed the continuity of humanity where people were trying to handle the issues of living life in the stresses of the polarity of love and hatred, poverty and superabundance, kindness and violence, power and powerlessness, in the interface between the local and the global. Maybe Caesarea is not so far below the surface as we might imagine, and it is only one of a multitude of sites now uncovered for all to see. Archaeology has revealed the continuum of human existence and has made the past live again to allow us to touch its roots and its truth.

Research into comparative literature has been equally revealing. We have been able to see what were the prevailing attitudes to various types of writing and to know what was meant by 'story' and how various events and truths were recorded. We have become aware of how a story is shaped in its detail in order to highlight the points of true significance. No longer do we filter everything we read in order to try to remove all that we do not consider to be so-called 'facts'. We have realized that fact has limited reality until it is coloured by relationship. We ask, What has this fact got to do with me and those around me? In the comparative literature it is clear that the authors used every method to make us relate to these facts and be stirred by them into the appropriate actions – actions which would shape our lives for the better.

As you and I turn the millennium, we are the heirs of all this research. As Christians we can turn to the Scriptures – the Old Testament and the New Testament – and ask questions such as these:

- Why was this recorded and remembered?
- What event lies behind this statement?
- How does this passage highlight the significance of this event for us?
- How does this passage bring the past into the present with power?
- What must I do to respond to this passage?

Because of all this careful research we can with confidence declare that those who transmitted the text by copying it from hand to hand made every attempt to be very accurate. The general knowledge of how texts were transmitted[1] has been greatly assisted by the discovery of the Dead

Sea Scrolls, found in caves along the hills above the side of the Dead Sea between 1947 and the late 1960s. The writings themselves date from the period 250–175 BC. They were the treasures of refugees fleeing the Roman armies during the destruction of Jerusalem in AD 70. I have visited the Museum of the Scrolls in modern Jerusalem and have seen for myself the copy of the scroll of the Book of the Prophet Isaiah. What is remarkable for scholars and for us is how similar this text is to those which had been used by earlier scholars for the translations which we have in the English versions of the Scriptures. Previously the earliest complete Hebrew versions of the Old Testament could not be traced back further than the fifteenth century. The similarity between the earlier and later texts attests to the accuracy of the scribes down the years, and the sense that Scripture is a precious tradition to be preserved and handed on with care and not to be altered at the whim of the scribe. This attitude obviously persisted down the centuries and was the rule for Christian scribes as well as their Hebrew counterparts. Scribes knew that what they were copying was a physical link in a chain that stretched back to the original authors and events. Their spiritual awareness gave them a sense of preserving not only something important to ages past, but important for them and the future as well.

Earlier this century some scholars were very sceptical about the 'accuracy' of the material in the New Testament because research showed that the text was not finally brought together until the latter half of the second century AD, and that the first record of the whole New Testament as we know it was not found until the middle of the fourth century in the work of St Athanasius. This was obviously a shock to a generation who believed that the nearer the recording of an event to its happening, the more accurate it was. Further research has shown us that some of St Paul's Letters date from the early AD 50s, and that the Gospels were written a little before and a little after the crucial date of the Fall of Jerusalem in AD 70. It is clear that the Christian writings were addressed to communities of Christians who were already well aware of most of the historical events pertaining to Jesus, the Christ, and any inaccuracies would therefore be challenged and corrected by these communities. To look at a parallel situation in the 1980s and 1990s, we all have observed how 'old' people were well able to recall accurately (especially in a group situation of old neighbours or old soldiers) the striking events of the Second World War. Many of the memories of this global war were recorded for the first time in books some 50 years after the events took place. This is a comparable time span to that of the events of Jesus' life before the memories were sealed in the records that have finally come down to us. As in the case of the War, individuals often had notes written at the time and had rehearsed the stories of the events year by year on the anniversaries and during times of fellowship at reunions. The communities of those involved kept alive the sharp memories and refined the recollections to the essentials so that their deepest meaning was portrayed and preserved.

It was helpful to me to see in the Museum of the Scrolls in Jerusalem the number of small papyri and fragments which contained personal messages such as bills, letters and instructions. These seem to have been part of the social system of an age parallel to the formation of the earliest Christian writings.

All this one can say is 'history', but it is important for Christians to regain their confidence in the declaration of their history. It has now stood up to the test of rigorous investigation and can be put into a wide context of knowledge. This allows us to overcome the reserve of Christians in the century just passing, who feared that the historical basis of their faith could not be sustained. The events surrounding the time of the Incarnate Christ seemed to them to have been shrouded in such mists that they were best relegated to mystery and imagination. Now we no longer need to hide them away as an embarrassment, but can again claim them as the true foundation of the Christian Faith. Jesus of Nazareth did live some 2000 years ago. Much of what was significant in his life and death is recorded for us. His disciples did attest to his Resurrection and Ascension, and the Church born of his Spirit did expand to proclaim the Good News of his disclosure of the nature and activity of God.

Another cause of the return of confidence in Christians is the reawakening of the understanding that 'man (humanity) cannot live by bread alone'. Many have come to realize the bankruptcy of materialism. The discoveries of science led to an attitude of the priority of the tangible over the intangible. What was seen through the microscope was deemed to be more valid than what was observed through intuition or experience. The world came to be focused on cause and effect, and all causes had to be limited to the material. Thus sickness was considered the result of the cause of visible organisms. The non-material causes were often ignored, such as stress, removal of dignity, or the loss of a sense of purpose. Healing was attributed to medicine or surgery, and the contribution of a sense of wellbeing and peace was mostly ignored. Such restrictive attitudes are fast disappearing, if they have not vanished altogether. Now a 'holistic' approach to life and learning is encouraged as essential to truth and wellbeing.

It has also become obvious during the twentieth century that knowledge and material comfort will not in themselves provide happiness and fulfilment. In fact they may not even contribute to a quality of 'goodness'. Clever people have no guarantee of happiness, and rich people have suffered greatly from depression, feeling valued only for their money, which they know does not dictate their sense of worth. Thus there has been an upsurge in the search for spiritual values. This has given rise to the search for 'miracles and wonders' as well as a mature, balanced response to the Divine outpouring of grace. Whatever the form, popular sentiment has seen through the bankruptcy of the material, and the futility of chasing the gold at the end of the rainbow. We hear that even some casinos are down on their luck and facing bankruptcy, like so many of the winners of a so-called fortune!

In the face of this new hunger of the spirit, how can Christians confidently point to the experience of the Spirit of God as the true way to find 'wholeness', and to maintain their life in a balanced perspective? In response to that question, Christians have the great advantage of being able to affirm both the material and the spiritual. The Creation and the Incarnation of Jesus Christ both affirm that God takes the material of this world seriously and defines it as important for God's purposes. The Creation about us is to be seen as the place in which all creatures live, move and have their being. As we now know all too well as we draw nigh to the end of this millennium, the created order is delicately balanced. It cannot be exploited or ignored in our decision-making. Human beings cannot treat the created order as a possession to be turned into a cash crop for the greedy. If one generation takes more from it than is needful, then future generations will be deprived of the essentials of life. In the created order there is a spirit of generosity, but also a spirit which can be destroyed by violent exploitation. The trees and plants have a necessary place within it, not only for material purposes, but also for spiritual purposes. They provide the oxygen-recycling factory on the one hand, their fruits provide food and seed at the same time, and the larger ones provide the source of shelter and warmth. On the other hand, trees and plants bring forth a beauty which delights the soul, giving us a sense of continuity with the past and the future, and show forth colours both for restfulness and vibrancy which stimulate the senses. I could write similar sentiments for the animal kingdom, for the birds and insects, and even for the sky and the sea. The Creation provides food for the soul as well as for the body.

The year 2000 and the beginning of the new millennium will see renewed efforts by Christians to affirm their belief in God as Creator, and they will resolve afresh to care for Creation as part of their relationship with the Creator. Christians will see the spiritual importance of this as well as the material. The breakdown in the ecosystem has been a useful reminder that an egocentric attitude by humanity is destructive not only in itself, but also to the Creation as a whole. It is obvious that if human beings usurp the place of God at the centre and try to take control of the universe in order to organize Creation for the profit of humankind, such a policy is self-defeating. Human beings are under the same rules as the rest of the created order, and cannot make up the rules to suit themselves. It is a fact, not a threat, that the sins of the parents will be visited on the children in this respect. Sustainability and mutual respect are the key attitudes set down by the Creator for all creatures for their spiritual as well as their material wellbeing. In this case Christians join with those who strive to preserve the created order, while at the same time proclaiming the Gospel message that nature as well as humanity is capable of redemption on the same terms as we all receive salvation – a humility to seek forgiveness and renewal, and a trust in the Spirit of God who is the centre and purpose of all living things. Such a principle raises the possibility of living again under a new pattern of existence – a true resurrection. So Christians add to the Creation debate not only the call to repentance but also the hope of renewal.

The second contribution that Christians can confidently make to the search for wholeness of life and a proper balance between the material and the spiritual is their witness to the Incarnation of the Son of God in the birth of Jesus Christ. That God became fully human in the life of Jesus of Nazareth is an article of faith, born out of historical testimony and spiritual experience. The effrontery of this statement to a scientific generation is that it cannot be explained in material terms. To them human and Divine are seen as exclusive, not inclusive, terms. Thus Jesus has to be one or the other from a material point of view. Some have solved the dilemma by denying the existence of Jesus altogether. They get rid of the 'problem' by eliminating the person, which is a very dangerous attitude to people. But history and faith have stubbornly refused to wipe out Jesus. Even the year 2000 keeps him alive in the minds of the global village. More people on earth know of or possess the Book which contains the record of his existence than any other single book. Jesus still walks the earth with the significance of his Spirit, his memory, and his message for humanity.

The Incarnation is the supreme witness that in God the material and the spiritual can exist in perfect fullness and harmony. Here the Divine and the human are intertwined in the ultimate both/and statement. In this

Incarnation God gives us the model for our existence. The event of the Incarnation of Christ is indeed unique, which is why it is so important to celebrate the year 2000 with fullness and joy. There is no other Divine/human person besides Jesus, the Christ. However, it is the matter of degree which marks out Jesus as unique. The principle is inherent in us all to *some* extent. All those who share his Spirit and are members of his community experience the gift of the Holy Spirit, the Divine life, within our material existence. But this is not yet in full measure, and is certainly not ours by our own power. It is achieved by the gift and generosity of the Divine power, of the Godhead itself. As our life grows in the power of his life, so the Divine develops in us to create a balanced whole where the spiritual (the Godlike) and the material (the human) live together in mutual interdependence.

Every Christmas season Christians, and many others who are touched by the story, demonstrate the history of the Incarnation and the power of its significance as they put into practice in their lives the spirit of Christmas. The story as it was in history is remembered and retold in such a way as to affect our present time and practice. Each birth of a baby becomes a gift and not a nuisance or a cause of exploitation. Each child is raised to a position of dignity. It was not coincidence that the leaders who challenged and still challenge child exploitation were Christians dedicated to fulfil the teaching of the child born at Bethlehem. In the light of that birth, no child can be just a material object to be used for profit or pleasure or parental support. No child can be discarded as surplus to requirements. Every child henceforth is of spiritual significance and of Divine potential. This is the message of the Incarnation by which God has fully identified with all humanity, from the youngest to the oldest, from the most frail to the most powerful.

The Incarnation is also to be celebrated as the full disclosure of the Divine Word. Christians speak their words to proclaim that God has spoken fully in Jesus Christ. The communication of the Word is both by Spirit and by flesh. Christians have experienced how the inner soul converses with the Divine Word. In meditation and in worship God's Spirit joins with our spirit in revealing the true nature of the relationship. But we are not left in the realm of mystery, wondering whether our thoughts and the message of God have become confused. Because of the Incarnation we have a physical voice to be heard as well as the inner voice of the soul. Jesus conveys in word and action the truth about God, about the will of God, and about the way we enter into, maintain and reconnect our relationship with the Godhead.

Those who deny the fully Divine/human aspect of the Incarnation remove the litmus test of truth that the event gives to us. If Jesus is not fully human, he cannot understand humanity sufficiently to communicate 'from the inside'. If he is not fully Divine, then the message does not come from the source itself but is simply hearsay, second-hand and open to reinterpretation.

The year 2000 gives Christians another opportunity to declare both the necessity and the truth of acknowledging the Incarnation. In the next chapter I will discuss the ambiguities of the time and place of such an Incarnation, but there is no reason at all for Christians to feel any lack of confidence in the fact of Jesus' existence, and the claims made by and about him. What may be new for many Christians is to proclaim this message to a generation which, as we have seen above, knows that communication is at the heart of relationships, that the events of the past do and can shape the future, that both the spiritual and the material coexist and must be kept in balance, and that to raise humanity to the place of God is dangerous and self-destructive. The new climate in the new millennium may well welcome the witness that Christians are ready to give out of their new-found knowledge and their continual experience.

What, then, will give Christians this confidence to celebrate the year 2000 and to witness to their faith? If we look at the way the first disciples of Christ handled the opportunity to witness to the events and experience of Christ in the record we call the Acts of the Apostles, we discover the frequent use of the word which in English is translated as 'boldness' (Acts 4:39; 9:27; 18:26 are examples). The word is used constantly in Acts 4, where the disciples Peter and John are recognized for the 'boldness' with which they tell the story of Jesus. They tell the Council of Leaders sitting in judgement over them that 'we cannot keep from speaking about what we have seen and heard' (v. 20). After their release with a warning that they are to stop preaching, the two pray for boldness with the words: 'grant to your servants to speak your word with all boldness' (v. 29). This prayer was answered as 'they were all filled with the Holy Spirit and spoke the word of God with boldness' (v. 31). Later reference is made to St Paul's boldness in speaking about Jesus (Acts 9:27) and to that of the disciple Apollos, who 'spoke with burning enthusiasm and taught accurately the things concerning Jesus' (Acts 18:25). In one of his personal Letters St Paul uses the word 'boldness' in his plea to a fellow Christian to welcome a former slave back as his brother in Christ rather than as a runaway (Philemon 8).

This attitude of boldness is one which all Christians can use in the cele-bration of the year 2000. It is the result of confidence in God and in the vitality of the message about Jesus. Such boldness does not equate to arrogance because it is a gift which we are given, not a power which we possess for ourselves. The gift comes through the humility of prayer. We wait on God to inspire us with the right words to share our experience of God and our knowledge of the facts of Christ. It is born in us out of the Holy Spirit's power. It is the outcome of our relationship with God. It is therefore a boldness which respects the listener but has no hesitancy about the truth of the news and views which we share. For Christians the facts of the past are supported by the experience of the present.

It is never enough to say what the Scriptures and the Church declare about Jesus of Nazareth. The message needs to be supported by the living experience of the speaker. First they will tell the truth about the birth, life, death, resurrection and ascension of Jesus Christ. Then they will go on to tell with boldness the significance of the message for the present life of the speaker. To be true to their calling, Christians must have both knowledge and experience in full harmony. When we speak of the Incarnation of Jesus Christ 2000 years ago, this will be supported by our witness as to how Jesus has been born in our life through faith. This experience will be both spiritual and material. It is not a balanced view just to point to the good deeds that have been inspired by the coming of Jesus. Mother Teresa, one of the saints of the twentieth century, was admired for her good deeds among the dying and the poor, but above all she was attractive to so many for fully combining this with her holiness and her spirituality which came forth in her prayers, her humility and her words of wisdom. In her the Divine/human integration was revealed. And yet all the time she witnessed to her own need for a Saviour and her own reliance on the gifts of the Holy Spirit. It was the revelation of her experience which drew the listener to open their ears to her message – the value to God of the least significant to humankind; the truth of the promise of eternal life even to those who seemed most dead in the eyes of the world; the identification with all humanity as being neighbours in Christ so that when one suffers, we all suffer; and above all the care and the love of the Creator which Christ's love makes known to all people.

Mother Teresa was a saint of the age, but it is still true that the experience of the more usual Christian, with a life transformed in much quieter ways, will be shared with others as we celebrate the year 2000. We will speak of our own awareness of God, of the relationship that God has nurtured and encouraged in us as soon as we said our first hesitant 'yes' in response to God's initiative, of the growing sensitization of our conscience so that it became aware of new values and new ideals, of the ability to ask for forgiveness from God and others and of the joy of being forgiven, of the inner strength and courage to face the storms of life, of the deep peace in facing our losses and disappointments, and above all of growth towards the fulfilment of the will of God and the purpose of life which we know begins now and is completed in eternity.

I have discovered that some of the hesitation that Christians express in their witness to their faith is that they have no framework on which to build the basic message about Christianity, especially to a generation which has a very sketchy understanding of what Christians believe and do. I was personally faced with such a situation when I was asked to give a lecture for an hour or so to a group of students who were studying the various religious views held in their community as part of a degree and diploma course for those entering the advertising and communication fields of work. How could I give them a framework to introduce them to Christianity? This is what I shared with them:

AN INTRODUCTION TO CHRISTIANITY

When trying to understand any religion it is good to ask a number of key questions:

- What do they believe about God?
- What do they believe about human beings?
- What do they do to worship God?
- What do they do to respect other human beings?
- What do they believe about themselves?

Christianity, like other religions, starts with the assumption that there is a Divine Power or Being in the Universe which is more than the sum of individuals' thinking. Religion is about the 'Other' as well as about 'us'. So the language of religion contrasts the human with the Divine.

Humanism is the name we give to the assumption that everything and everyone can be limited to humanity; and that the centre of all things is the human being, who possesses the power to make the achievements that he or she considers desirable. In the light of human behaviour in the twentieth century, we would probably now regard this assumption as arrogant and dangerous.

Religion is the name we give to the assumption that the Divine is greater than the human and in some sense is responsible for the created order.

What do Christians believe about God?

Christians believe:

- That God exists in a state of ongoing being.
- That God created the whole Universe with the purpose of relating to all things.
- That God's purpose in that relationship is to reveal the being of God to humanity and to seek a free response to God's approach of love.
- That to fulfil this purpose, God has inspired women and men in every age with the knowledge of the Divine and has given to every human being the capacity to grasp this knowledge.
- That at a chosen point in history God revealed the being of God to humanity in a total commitment of love by coming into human existence in a particular person called Jesus of Nazareth. This Jesus fully possessed the being and mind of God, and took human nature so that he could communicate with humanity on an equal basis. Jesus revealed God as wanting a relationship with all people of every age, gender and race, and even being ready to renew this relationship through forgiveness when human beings tried to destroy the relationship by killing him.
- That Jesus made clear that even death could not separate us from the relationship with God, and that resurrection to a life beyond physical death was a reality for God's Creation.
- That the presence and power of God was able to be experienced through the Spirit of Jesus which was given to all who believed in him.
- That those who possess the Spirit of God are bound together into a fellowship of mutuality which is like an extended family of which Jesus is the Head. This fellowship keeps the presence of Christ real for its members and is the means of witness and service to the rest of humanity.

What do Christians believe about human beings?

Christians believe:

- That each human being is part of the created order and has a special responsibility to be accountable to the Creator God for the care of Creation.

- That each human being is unique and equal in the sight of God, and has been given gifts of personality and talents to be used for the welfare of the whole human race.
- That each human being is capable of responding to the love of God and of entering into a full relationship with the Creator.
- That human beings are capable of caring and supporting one another and finding true fulfilment by doing so.
- That out of God's love for humanity, Jesus Christ came to model for human beings the way to live with confident trust, despite the risks and hazards of the Universe.
- That human beings possess the gifts of reason and communication, and can therefore determine the best course of action unless corrupted by selfishness, insecurity or greed.
- That human beings can be so filled with the Spirit of God that they reflect in their lives the true nature of God, even though they must never attempt to become God themselves.
- That human beings are free to reject God, but by doing so cut themselves off from the source of life in all its fullness.

What do Christians do to worship God?

- Christians see worship as one of the main responses in their relationship with God. To worship God is to acknowledge that God is the primary focus in the life of a Christian, and that the relationship is of supreme importance. In worshipping God, Christians find that they feel valued themselves and enjoy entering into the relationship.
- Because worship is an activity of the whole person – spiritual and physical combined – the body as well as the mind and spirit is involved.
- Christians worship by ritual (movements repeated to express meaning), through symbol (an outward object that conveys a spiritual meaning by association), and through word and silence.
- Strong emotions and precious memories are held by those who worship. Music and movement are aids to such feelings.
- Worship is a corporate activity as well as an individual action. Therefore Christians have provided corporate space for occasions of worship and connect this space with an experience of the presence of God. These spaces are called shrines or churches as appropriate. Within these spaces there are 'holy objects' which also express the presence of God. These objects include symbols, art, furniture, statues and books.

- The most common symbol is a Cross, whose meaning is attached to the victory of love that Jesus the Christ accomplished at the event of his crucifixion by the Roman occupying army in Jerusalem in about AD 33. The symbol stands for the ability of God to forgive the worst of human rejection and for the means of drawing all people back into a relationship with God. The Cross is also a warning about what human beings do to others if they reject God and live in hatred and selfishness.
- The most common piece of furniture is a table which is used for the Communion Meal, when bread and wine are shared among Christians as symbols of the continuing presence of Christ among them.
- At the centre of the collection of books is the sacred Scripture, known as the Bible. It reveals the record of God's actions and communication with humanity, particularly through the Israelite people and the first followers of Jesus the Christ.

What do Christians do to respect other human beings?

Because Christians have found their worth and purpose through their worship of God, they feel empowered by God to care for other human beings as of supreme value to God. This care extends to moral, spiritual and practical support.

- Christians seek to share with all other people the Good News of their Faith and particularly what God has done in the life, death and resurrection of Jesus Christ.
- Christians seek to make real the goal of Creation as a place of harmony, reconciliation and fulfilment, where all things are in balance and all things needful for life are sustained.
- Christians work for peace and justice between the peoples of the world so that each person is established as of worth to the whole, and oppression, war and exploitation are banished.
- Christians are involved in the cure of the sick, in the care of the dying, and in the feeding of the hungry. Such compassion, accompanied by a hope in the resurrected life, is empowered by the Spirit of Jesus, who acted in like manner while on earth.

What do Christians believe about themselves?

Christians believe:

- That they can respond to God and enter into a full relationship in which the primacy of God and the holiness of God are acknowledged.
- That they have been given free will by God and are therefore called to live responsibly. They know that they can misuse the gifts that they have been given, and become selfish and capable of destroying themselves and others. They 'repent' of (turn away from) the evil they do and believe that they can trust God to forgive them as Jesus forgave those who killed him on the Cross.
- That the Spirit of God enters into their being so that they are empowered to live and act in accordance with the goals set before them by the teaching of Jesus and the application of such teaching by the 'mind' of the Church.
- That they live in an orderly Creation, and that they can discover how the Creation works and apply such knowledge for the benefit of all humanity. They believe that the Spirit of God reveals the truth through study and that the Spirit guides ethical choices.
- That they can be confident in their abilities but must be realistic about the failures in human nature. They value living in community where they find fellowship, mutual support and the opportunity to keep present the memory of Jesus.
- That this earthly life comes to its conclusion at death, and that there is a life beyond death when the limitations of mortality are overcome. In this further life, the 'person' continues to be unique and there is a continuity between the personality of the individual on earth and that in eternal life. Such eternal life is open to all who respond to God's offer of a full relationship with the Divine.
- That there will be a final 'summation' (fulfilment) for each person as well as for the whole Universe, when total wholeness, peace and goodness will be achieved.

Summary

Christianity is a religion in which the spiritual and the material are recognized; the Divine is seen as personal and unified; humanity is seen as potentially good within an ordered Universe created for a purpose; the Divine has entered fully into the human condition; and God has revealed the nature of the Divine to all people in the hope that they will respond to the relationship with love.

With such knowledge and our own experience, we will be able to share our faith with a boldness given to us by the Spirit in response to prayer. What will probably surprise us is the eagerness of our listeners to hear more from us. Some may dismiss us as idealists or as too spiritual in comparison to the possibilities they see for themselves. Yet many will thank us with joy for lighting with our spark their spiritual fire – long dormant or never lit – and together with us will give thanks to God in worship and praise. In us they will have met a soul friend who helped them make sense of the puzzles and removed the obstacles created by false information, bad experiences of Christians, through ridicule or through fear and loss. Those who respond will, like Mary at the well at Nazareth, whisper 'Yes', not knowing where it will end, but trusting God for the journey from the depth of their souls.

Now it is right to go back to our roots, to Nazareth and Bethlehem, to discover the events which started these millennium dates and the Faith which caused later leaders to redefine the turning point of history as the birth of the Christ Child.

2

OUR ROOTS
AT NAZARETH

I am writing this chapter on a calm and sunny New Year's Day. Early in the morning I saw the dawn, and later witnessed the sunrise. Such a day inspires the mind to give thanks for the past and to pray for the future. As the year turns, we ask again how we arrived at this point of time, where our roots began, and where we are going. Such thoughts will be all the sharper on the dawn of the year 2000. Then not only the year will change, but also the century and the millennium.

It was not until I did some research[1] that I was able to answer the question as to how we have our present dating system, why it is the year 2000, and who decided that it should be so. Knowing this helps us to put our history into place and to trace our roots. When I am looking to find the origins of my family history, there are three factors I must take into account – dates, people and places.

DATES

Let's look first at the dating system that is currently widely in use in the world. It was devised by a certain Dionysius, who gave himself the title of 'Exiguus' to distinguish himself from many others of the same name. Dionysius was a Scythian monk who lived in the late fifth and early sixth centuries. Scythians were an Indo-European people who lived between the Danube and the Don rivers and later spread out over the territory between the Caucasus mountains and the Caspian Sea. Traditionally tall of build and fierce of temperament, they were a strong and proud people who lived on the eastern borders of the Roman Empire.

Shortly after the death of Pope Gelasius I in AD 496 (as we would calculate it now), Dionysius was called to work at Rome. There he was asked to construct a new cycle of dates for the great Christian Festival of Easter for each of the years to come. The system of dating which was current at that time reckoned the number of each year as starting from the date of the accession of the Roman Emperor Diocletian over 200 years previously. Diocletian had created an absolute monarchy and concentrated all power on himself as a semi-divine ruler, leaving little authority in the hands of the old Roman Senate. He saw his accession as the beginning of a new age and the turning point in the history of humanity. At the beginning of his reign Christians, who were widely spread throughout the Empire, mostly enjoyed freedom from persecution such as they had suffered from time to time under every emperor. However, some 20 years after his accession, a great persecution of Christians, both clergy and laity, took place throughout the various regions of the Empire. This wave of persecution only came to an end 10 years later with the victory of Constantine, who was the first emperor to give full support to Christianity in return for its support of his power.

In view of this history, it is not hard to see why Dionysius should seize the opportunity not only to set the dates of Easter but also to put forward a new proposal as to how to number each year. He made a symbolic change to remove the memory of Diocletian and the persecutions from the record. He dated the first year in the Easter Cycle from what he believed was the dawn of a new age and the turning point in human history – the date of the Incarnation of Jesus Christ, the King of Kings and Lord of Lords. So the year 248 after the accession of Diocletian was replaced by the year 532 'from the Incarnation of our Lord Jesus Christ'. Using the Latin language, such a date came to be written '*Anno Domini* 532' (i.e. '532 years from the Incarnation of our Lord Jesus Christ'). This was then shortened to 'AD 532'.

We have no record of the method that Dionysius used to calculate the date for the birth of Christ, but what is remarkable is that some 500 and more years after the event, which had taken place in a rather obscure part of the known world, he was so accurate. All modern scholars, after years of accumulated research, believe that Dionysius was within four to six years of the most likely date. This indicates to me that the Christian community were very careful to keep alive their traditions and knew their own history in such a way as to be able to trace it back to their roots.

The scheme that Dionysius proposed was accepted, and it gradually spread outwards from Rome. We know from the records of the English historian St Bede that it was adopted in Britain by the Synod of Whitby in AD 664 and was also widespread at that time on the Continent of Europe. At the Synod of Whitby the customs of the Church in Rome prevailed over the earlier traditions of the Celtic Church in Scotland, Ireland and Northern England. We may have some sad feelings at the loss of cultural roots in this decision, but the common date for Easter did bring unity and the removal of deep hostility among Christians in Britain and Ireland at this time.

Modern scholarship has not the benefit of oral tradition only 500 years old, so it has had to rely on comparative written sources from the time of Jesus' birth, and from the discovery of inscribed stones revealed by archaeology. We need to remember that the birth of Jesus was not seen by the Early Church as equal in importance to the passion, death and resurrection of Jesus. The dating for these key events could be set in reference to the part played in them by Pontius Pilate. There is plenty of evidence that he was prefect of Judea and therefore the chief Roman authority in the years AD 26–36. Because of this, most scholars set the date of the crucifixion either in AD 30 or in AD 33. Such a date is supported by the reference in Luke's Gospel (3:23) that Jesus was 30 when he was baptized by John and began his public ministry.

In the New Testament the events surrounding the birth of Jesus are told only at the beginning of the Gospels of Matthew and Luke.[2] Both record the birth as taking place at a time when certain authorities were in power. Matthew refers to Herod the Great. Herod was a ruler who held a position of power in Judea as a vassal king under the authority of the Romans. Matthew begins his record (chapter 2) with the words: 'In the time of King Herod, after Jesus was born in Bethlehem of Judea …' and goes on to describe the conversation about the birth of Jesus between Herod and the Astrologers looking for a child who has been born King of the Jews. At that point of time Herod is obviously still alive and so fearful for his throne that he must give orders to kill any possible rivals. By Matthew 2:19 Herod is dead and his son Archelaus is ruling in his place. External documents record that Herod died in 4 BC, so if this dating is followed Jesus must have been born between about 7 and 4 BC, allowing up to two years to elapse between Jesus' birth and the visit of the Astrologers to the 'young child' (Matthew 2:16), and for some time in Egypt. This line of thinking has caused many scholars to put forward a date of about 6 BC for the birth of Jesus.

The references in Luke's Gospel are more complex but again put a date within the same decade. Luke sets the birth of John the Baptist 'in the days of King Herod of Judea' (Luke 1:5). Luke tells us (v. 36) of the visit of the angel for the annunciation to Mary, six months after John's conception. The assumption we can make from the Gospel record is that Jesus was also born 'in the days of King Herod'. However, Luke sets the birth of Jesus in the context of the Roman authorities of the time. He records that there was a census 'while Quirinius was governor of Syria'. We do know from other sources that a census was held from time to time in this period and that there was a major census in Palestine in AD 6 under Quirinius. However, that is too late a date to fit into the framework of Herod's reign. In his time the governor of Syria was Suturninus (9–6 BC), and it is note-worthy that a very early Christian writer, Tertullian (AD c. 160 – c. 220), also mentions the census in relation to the nativity but says the governor was Saturinus. The explanation for this uncertainty may be that Luke followed an early source. It may be that when the birth occurred, Mary and Joseph were in Bethlehem to register in a census 'like the census held in the time of Quirinius', one that was more widely known. The ideas could then have overlapped and the census could be said to be the later one. It is unlikely that we shall ever be certain of what caused the complexity in Luke's Gospel. What is in accordance with both Gospels is that Jesus was born at Bethlehem and later lived in Nazareth in a period of time about 2000 years ago. When tracing the roots of our ancestors we often have to accept that there are pieces of information which are lacking, and some which we have to leave to future generations in the hope that some clue to the missing facts will be uncovered. Even when we get very close to the detail but cannot go further, we never doubt the existence of the person we are tracing and the sense of history that the search brings.

PEOPLE

In our search for our roots we look for records not only of dates but also of earlier generations. The Maori people of New Zealand take great pride in being able to trace and know by heart their *whakapapa*. This is the line of their ancestors back to the founding chief or leader of the tribe. In both the Gospels of Luke and Matthew there is a similar genealogy for Jesus. Matthew traces the names from Abraham to Joseph, 'the husband of Mary, of whom Jesus was born' (Matthew 1:16). As is often the way in genealo-gies, the key people are recorded to give additional honour to the current generation. Matthew includes five women in his list, each of whom in a strange way is part of the purpose of God in providing a true leader for God's people. The last of the five is Mary, who takes precedence over her husband Joseph, defining him by her role as the Mother of the Messiah rather than the more usual reverse. Her inclusion prepares for the opening of the record of the birth:'When his mother Mary ...' (Matthew 1:18).

Matthew begins the list of Jesus' ancestors with the name of Abraham, not because Matthew wishes to restrict the work of the Messiah to the Hebrew people, but because God promised to Abraham that 'in you all the families of the earth shall be blessed' (Genesis 12:3). Abraham is the pioneer ancestor of all who journey in faith to respond to the call of God. In this there is a parallel with the Magi, who also journey from the East to find the promised land and the presence of God in the birth of a child descended from David. Abraham becomes the spiritual ancestor of all who seek God's anointed. One of these is Joseph, who takes centre-stage in the record of Jesus' birth in Matthew's Gospel. The evangelist does not claim that Joseph is the natural father of Jesus, but he does make it clear that Joseph, by naming Jesus, claims him as his son. This is the implication of the verse (Matthew 1:21): 'She [Mary] will bear a son, and you [Joseph] are to name him Jesus.' Jesus would become a member of Joseph's family, of the line of the great ancestors David and Abraham. Matthew shows how Joseph fulfils his part in this relationship. He will protect the child and provide a home for the family in Mary's home district of Nazareth, rather than in his home town of Bethlehem in the more dangerous region of Judea.

Joseph is given full honour in the opening chapters of the Gospel, but from then on there are very few references to him. Matthew records that Joseph was a *tekton* – a skilled craftsman in wood and maybe also in stone (Matthew 13:55); and Mark (Mark 6:3) indicates that Jesus took up his father's role and became a carpenter before beginning his public ministry. Carpenters were no doubt in demand in northern Galilee, where people flourished in the towns supported by the fertile valley of Jezreel and the resources from the Sea of Galilee. Recent archaeology has uncovered elaborate buildings and artefacts at Zippori from the first century BC to later Roman times. This city sued for peace with the Romans when they were using great severity to suppress the Jewish revolt in the area between AD 66 and AD 73. Much of it was therefore saved from destruction, and the digging has revealed the amazing talents and skills of local craftsmen. This was not the only prosperous city in the north, and with such opportunities the carpenter Joseph and later Jesus may have found much work in the district. The lack of subsequent references in the Gospels could well be explained by the death of Joseph some time before Jesus' public ministry. Mark and Matthew both mention Mary and a series of brothers and sisters in the context of Jesus' visit to his home town of Nazareth (Mark 6:3; Matthew 13:55–56). In John's Gospel there is reference to Jesus as 'the son of Joseph, whose father and mother we know' (John 6:42). Yet this verse does not necessarily imply that Joseph is still alive at this point in the story. It is possible that Jesus had to take over the place and work of Joseph when he died, and that he delayed the start of his ministry until his brothers were able to support the family.

We can leave our focus on Joseph at that point and turn our attention to Mary. She has a pivotal place in the story as it is told in Luke's Gospel. There Luke prepares for the birth of Jesus by telling us the story of Mary's cousin Elizabeth and her husband Zechariah. This sets the scene for the central role of Mary. It is to her at Nazareth that the annunciation takes place (Luke 1:26); her 'yes' signals the obedience of humanity to God's plan; she visits her cousin – not near Galilee but in a hill town in Judea, which would be one of the villages near Jerusalem like Bethlehem, Emmaus or Bethany (Luke 1:39, 65); Mary sings her song of praise for the initiatives of God in the care of people; she gives birth to her first-born at Bethlehem, where the shepherds come to worship him; she hears the hard prophecy about her son from the lips of Simeon in the Temple on the occasion of his circumcision; and she asks Jesus why, as a twelve-year-old boy, he ignored his parents' anxiety and lingered in the Temple discussing matters with the teachers there.

In John's Gospel we find Mary accompanying Jesus to a wedding at Cana, a small village not far from Nazareth, and later to Capernaum on the northern shores of the large Lake of Galilee. At the time of the crucifixion of Jesus, that Gospel indicates that Mary (his mother) and her sister Mary, the wife of Clopas, as well as Mary Magdalene were standing near the Cross (John 19:25). From the Cross Jesus asked one of his disciples – the one whom he loved – to care for his mother. The Gospel states: 'And from that hour the disciple took her into his own home' (v. 27). This fairly late Gospel shows how it was remembered that Jesus did not reject his family in spite of earlier recorded opposition from them to his ministry. Even in his greatest point of need he demonstrated his care for his mother and the place she had in his life and heart.

Luke, in his second volume of the proclamation and expansion of the Christian Faith (the Acts of the Apostles), tells us that Mary and Jesus' brothers formed part of the gathering of disciples in Jerusalem in the times immediately after the resurrection (Acts 1:14).

As we celebrate the year 2000 it is right that Mary should have a place of honour among those whom we will remember with thanksgiving for their place in the Christian story. Mary not only gave birth to the Saviour but also followed his journey to the Cross and the grave, and shared in his resurrection promise of new life and new hope for all people. Luke makes clear in his genealogy that every human being shares in the hope that Jesus brought. He traces the ancestry back to 'Adam, the son of God' (Luke 3:38). In this symbolic way Jesus is declared to be the brother of all humanity, whatever gender, race and culture we claim. Every person can find their roots in this Jesus, Son of God and son of Adam.

PLACES

Places of significance also have a major part in finding our roots.[3] So far in this chapter I have made mention of Nazareth, Bethlehem and Jerusalem. I have included a map (see opposite page) so that readers will have some idea of the geographical context of this story.

The first thing to remember when looking at a map of this part of the world is its relative size. This is a small slice of the world, but it has always been of major significance. It is a place of struggle and tension, being a crossroads that a number of nations over the years have claimed for themselves. It is still a divided country in terms of cultures, faith and ethnic connections. The most northern point touched by our story is Mount Hermon, which overlooks the Golan Heights and touches on the borders of modern Lebanon and Syria. The top of the range is over 9000 feet, and in winter its slopes are used for skiing. The southern boundary of the land is at the bottom of a V-shaped area of mostly desert where is located the resort town of Eilat, at the apex of the Red Sea gulf. The distance from north to south is some 400 kilometres (about 300 miles). As far as width is concerned, it is a very narrow strip of territory lying between the Mediterranean Sea coast and the deep rift of the Jordan valley leading down to the Dead Sea and beyond. At its widest point, between the Gaza Strip and the lower Dead Sea desert area, the distance is about 100 kilometres (63 miles), and at its most narrow point, from Haifa to the Sea of Galilee, the distance is about 50 kilometres (31 miles). So we can compare it in overall size (not shape) to Wales in Great Britain or Massachusetts in the USA or Hawke's Bay in New Zealand.

When I visited this land we were driven by coach in a morning from Jerusalem in the centre down to the mountain fortress at Masada

Map of the modern state of Israel and the territory
under the Palestinian authority

overlooking the Dead Sea, passing Qumran, where the Scrolls were found, on the way. After a swim and then a lunch-break half way up the Dead Sea, in the afternoon we travelled up the divide to the ancient city of Jericho and along the borders of the Jordan River. By the late afternoon we were standing at the lookout near the demilitarized zone, gazing towards Damascus from the Golan Heights, with Mount Hermon visible above us. We had time to drop down towards the border with Lebanon before reaching our kibbutz for dinner and an overnight stay. We had stopped at key places on the way and were tired at the end of the journey, but it was all accomplished in one day. This gives you some idea of the distances in this small country, so rich in history and subject to so many changes over the years.

Even now the countryside is full of dramatic contrasts. There is the hilly nature of Jerusalem and its surrounding villages, some 2000 feet above sea level. Then there is the hot, dry wilderness land around the Dead Sea 1300 feet below sea level – hot, brown and parched when I was there in early September. In contrast, there was the shade and freshness of the River Jordan, tumbling over rocks to form perfect pools and overhung by soft, green trees. Its deep, green waters were in contrast to the fickle waves of the Sea of Galilee into which it flowed. This Sea was as smooth as glass as we approached and it reflected the surrounding hills that swept down to its shores. Crossing the lake later, we experienced its white, cresting waves as the wind roared down the folds between those same hills. Sacred memories came to mind as we sailed on these waters, watching the fish below and the storm-clouds above, like Peter, Andrew, James and John. We had begun our boat journey at the old imperial centre of Tiberias and completed it near Capernaum, Peter's home town on the lakeside.

The shoreline of the Mediterranean is different again, with its cooling breeze, its surf and long stretches of sand, broken only with deep water at Akko and Haifa in the north to provide safe harbours for shipping. In contrast, the inland sands of the desert in the south shimmer in the sunshine, relieved only now and again by the occasional lush oasis. On the edges of the dry parts modern irrigation has made the desert bloom, but only at the expense of lessening the flow of water out of the Lake of Galilee (the fresh-water reservoir for the whole area) into the Jordan. The loss has reached such an extent that the lower part of the Dead Sea is continually shrinking. There the salt and the heat are intensifying and the lack of water shows that all development is at a price, and that the price here is water, the most precious commodity in this dry land. All the surrounding peoples are dependent on the river's resources, and if one country takes more than its share there is less for their neighbours. People fight over water in such circumstances.

In contrast, the rich, fertile plains of northern Galilee are a sight to behold in their dress of green. Crops are abundant and the skills of cultivators are visible for all to see. Here it is that the cooperative spirit in the kibbutzim is most evident. In the dry lands the pastoral farmers still tend their flocks and find them places of shade and still waters.

Sadly, signs of deep divisions in this land are also evident. To go from Jerusalem to Bethlehem, a car drive of some ten minutes, may take much longer because of the check-point on the way. Here the road leaves the area controlled by the Israeli government for that under the Palestinian authorities. At the crossing-point the guns and the different-coloured car registration plates are most obvious. Neighbours find it hard to live with one another as the issues over ties to the land cause two cultures to clash. Every metre of this land has a history, and two peoples claim it for their own different reasons. Tracing our Christian roots here is a painful as well as an exhilarating experience. It seems you cannot put your foot on the land without treading on someone's toes. In the end you say least and see most, drinking in the context and the contours as the source of biblical reflection. The words of Jesus become potent – 'Who is your neighbour?' (Luke 10:29); 'My peace I give to you, but not as the world gives it' (John 14:27, adapted). Even in the cafes in Jerusalem, the city of prophetic peace, the young women soldiers carry a bunch of flowers in one hand and an automatic rifle in the other.

With these few general impressions of this land, it is time to take you to the three key places we have mentioned – Nazareth, Bethlehem and Jerusalem.

In the morning light we travelled from Tiberias on Lake Galilee up the road that leads from there towards the Mediterranean coast through the hills of northern Galilee. Dropping up and down through the rolling countryside, we were soon passing through Cana, still a small village nestling among lands growing olives, grapes, pomegranates and figs. We knew from here it was only eight kilometres (five miles) to Nazareth, but I had not realized until then that it was such a hilly road to climb. We descended the hill into Nazareth to be quickly made aware of its modern bustle, not only from the buses carrying the tourists but also from the local population of some 70,000, many of whom were engaged in the automotive industry. This town is within the State of modern Israel, even though it is populated by Arab peoples – both Muslim and Christian. For many years the mayor here was a Christian. In recognition of this and the importance of tourism to the whole economy, the Government in 1969 provided the finance for the local Roman Catholic Church to erect a new church to be designed by an architect from Rome. It is called the Church of the Annunciation and is remarkable both for its size and for the artwork contained within and around it. It replaces many earlier churches built on this site.

On a sunny day in early September we climbed up the road from the village well (the only source of drinking water in earlier times). Opposite it there is the Greek Orthodox Church of Saint Gabriel in which there is a holy spring. At the top of the steep Casa Nova Street we reached the rose-tinted Church of the Annunciation, which is under the guardianship of the Franciscans. We entered through beautiful wrought-iron gates into a courtyard in front of the main entrance. Towering above was a tall, black-roofed dome surrounded by stonework in fine tracery that looked like a jewelled crown. We passed over marble floors to peer down into a grotto cave far below before which there was a stone altar. Pilgrims were kneeling in the grotto, recalling before the candles the annunciation to Mary that she should bear God's Son. Tradition has it that this is the very site of the house where Mary lived in this town of Nazareth. A greater crowd of pilgrims were gathering around the stone altar to celebrate the presence now of her Son, their Lord, made known to them in broken bread and outpoured wine.

We quietly withdrew from the railings to explore the upper floor which was the nave of the main church. It was some 70 yards long and 30 yards wide. The walls all around the edges were decorated with art from every culture. On one side of us was a Madonna and Child panel from Japan, dressed in beautiful kimonos of white and blue respectively. On the other side of the nave our eyes focused on two figures – a Mother and Child – portrayed symbolically in Mexican art using only the colours ochre and white. Beyond were stained-glass windows containing every colour and hue, and then mosaic in gold leaf and brilliant colours, all telling the story of the angel and the young girl, drawing back in fear and humility at such a great responsibility. Above the main altar was a fresco painting showing the Church of all ages gazing up to heaven where Christ, dressed in red, stretches out his arms in welcome to St Peter and all the saints, while behind him in blue is seated the Holy Mother on her throne of honour. As I turned I saw that seated below in front of the high altar were the modern pilgrims and saints 'from every nation, tribe and language', representing a worshipping multitude that no one could number.

We crossed another courtyard surrounded by date palms and cypresses to the Church of Saint Joseph. In a niche in a wall is a simple, touching family group carved in white stone. The young child Jesus is stepping out in front, supported by Mary with hands clasped in prayer, and by the practical Joseph carrying his protective staff. Beneath this older church there is a complex of hewn-rock chambers which are thought to have been the home of the holy family. To help us imagine the scene there is a mural of Joseph standing at the carpenter's bench helping the lad Jesus use a measuring rule, while Mary seated on a stool looks on.

Both churches and courtyards are filled with images of different styles, cultures and materials to help us focus on this turning point in history, when God chose to be part of a particular family so that we can all be gathered into one family with Christ as Head. The excellence of the art and craftsmanship reminds us not to dismiss this town of Nazareth as poor or backward, either now or 2000 years ago. The treasures of the present are there for all to see. The treasures of the past can be imagined from the uncovered riches and elaborate buildings at Bet She'an, a little south of Tiberias, and at Zippori, just a little to the north of Nazareth. The Creator of the world takes human nature as a craftsman of materials and of human hearts.

Like Mary and Joseph, we must travel from Nazareth in the north to Bethlehem in the hills of Judea in the centre of the country. There is a road (now Route 60) which runs between the Mediterranean Sea and the Jordan River down the middle of the land. It passes the towns of Afula and Jenin before reaching Nablus, also known by the older name of Shekhem. This is the site of the hill shrine of early Israel within the biblical territory of Samaria. From here it is a hilly run south through Ramallah to Jerusalem. Five miles further on to the south, still on Route 60, you reach Bethlehem if you have successfully negotiated the check-point. Most of the area through which you have travelled is part of the Palestinian West Bank territories. It is only as you pass through Jerusalem itself that you enter the territory of the State of Israel. In a direct line the distance from Nazareth to Bethlehem is about 100 kilometres or some 60 miles.

On a hot summer afternoon we drove into Manger Square, a large parking area in front of the Church of the Nativity. There has been a church continuously on this site since the one built in AD 330 by St Helen, the mother of the Emperor Constantine. It is one of the oldest churches in Christendom and was constructed over the place where, according to St Jerome (AD c. 342–420), the infant Jesus was believed to have been born in a cave. The current church complex contains spaces for the different Christian communities that want to remember the birth of Jesus here. The array of crosses on the roof tells it all. There is a Greek Orthodox cross, the Cross of St Francis, and the Cross of the Armenian Church.

As you pass into the building you have to humble yourself by bending low. Most of the large portico has been filled in with masonry and only a small wooden door at the bottom corner remains accessible. This is said to be for reasons of safety, so that heretic horsemen could not ride into the church and put the pilgrims to flight.

Once inside, you enter a large space edged by tall Corinthian columns with carved capitals. This is the Byzantine church. You can still see evidence of the original mosaic paving beneath your feet, and the walls above the columns have the outline of dim painted frescos. Indeed, this was a temple fit for a king. The front of the space of this church is now divided into areas for each of the users – part for the Orthodox and part for the Armenian. The areas are highly decorated with carved wooden walls, hanging chandeliers, painted icons and lots of hanging lamps. Those who appreciate ceremonial in worship will find treasure here.

However, those who look for mystery in simplicity will be more rewarded by moving to the grotto beneath the upper church. Here in the resemblance of a cave is a 14-pointed bronze star set in a marble floor and surrounded by many lamps. These words in Latin, telling us that here Jesus was born, are written with confident faith:

HIC DE VIRGINE MARIA
JESUS CHRISTUS NATUS EST.

On one side of this cave is an altar representing the manger. It is constructed of a mixture of marble slabs, but its simplicity is quite compelling. On the other side is an altar to commemorate the visit of the Three Kings. We stood there slightly stooped in the stillness and coolness of this holy spot. The generations of pilgrims who had gone before us were obvious in the ancient hangings and the well-worn pavements and trimmed lamps. Yes, here we were in touch with history, but we knew that the whole scene would not live unless there were lives transformed by beauty, vitality and peace. It was awesome, but also challenging. The stone of the cave might remember the cry of a baby, but it was up to us to breathe fresh life into Christ's message. We would have to be agents of renewal, messengers of peace, heralds of repentance and those who proclaimed God's salvation. We left the cave in search of air and light.

Connected to this grotto by a narrow passage, whose small door is kept locked for most of the year, is the parish church of Bethlehem for the

Roman Catholic community. It is dedicated to St Catherine, an early martyr whose death witnessed to the lordship of Christ in her life. Its high-vaulted roof and bright, sunlit interior was in contrast to the cave beneath. We entered silently and were drawn to kneel in prayer, noting others around us doing the same. We gave thanks for the birth of Christ, for the courage of Mary and Joseph, and for the way the seed of the Church had been born again in the blood of the martyrs. Then it was time to rise and join the rest of the group outside. As we left, the setting sun caught the colours in a circular window above the door. In it a star shone down upon the Child, held in the arms of his Mother and supported by Joseph. Before him knelt the Magi, offering their gifts to the infant king. We left Bethlehem as evening came. As we drove to Jerusalem we passed the shepherds' field, but there seemed to be more white houses on the slopes now than white lambs.

Jerusalem is a bustling city set on a series of hills. The old and the new jostle for space. Three of the world's great religions vie for position there, and their memorials commemorate death as well as life. For Christian pilgrims searching for their roots the city contains the sites of the Last Supper, the Passion, the Crucifixion and the Resurrection. On a hillside opposite the Temple site stands the Mount of Olives, the point of entry on Palm Sunday and the place of exit at the Ascension. The current tensions within the city are as palpable as in the time of Christ. Soldiers still carry weapons in the streets; in the dark, narrow passages people still walk hurriedly as if afraid of a furtive attack; the Muslim on the Dome of the Rock still eyes with deep suspicion his Jewish neighbour at the Wailing Wall far below; and even rival Christian groups sharing the holy sites have been known to raise fists or weapons at one another over the breaking of some rule laid down to keep the peace. The current pilgrim feels the same attraction and the same caution that Jesus felt for this holy city.

We saw it first from the Mount of Olives on a clear early morning, with the sun shining over our backs onto the gold-plated Dome of the Rock, now standing on the site where once the Temple had stood. We walked down a steep path to the Kidron Valley and found ourselves among the olive trees in the Garden of Gethsemane. Many trees looked as old as 2000 years, thickened in the trunk by pruning over the centuries. Alongside the trees we entered the Church of All Nations built around a great basalt rock. There, gathered from all nations, we offered our obedience to Christ who had gained strength beside this rock to face the Cross for the salvation of the world.

We climbed the Via Dolorosa in the midday heat and were glad that we only had to carry our water bottles and not a cross. The stones on either side seemed to cry out and the crowds still pressed in upon us as they hurried on their way in the narrow passages. Flagging in energy, we reached the final Stations of the Cross in the Church of the Holy Sepulchre, and later entered the tomb there. By now our emotions were raw and we kept asking ourselves the question: 'Are we any closer to Christ here than we are in our own country and church community?'

'Yes and no' was the ambivalent answer. Yes, in the sense that the physical presence was unavoidable. The Passion climb to Calvary's Cross was painful and pressing. The tomb was the reality of death. Outside it I longed to write the words: 'He is not here, he is risen!' Yes, more clearly than ever we understood the feelings of tension and oppression. How aware we now were of leaving the walled city and finding the contrasting space and uplift of the top ridge of the Mount of Olives – the place of the Ascension. Everything was a physical reality for us now.

But no, Christ was made just as real for us in the lives of people we had met – in the dedication of the frail Franciscan nuns at the Church of the Beatitudes overlooking the Galilean Lake; in the devotion of the pilgrims at Mass in the Church of the Annunciation at Nazareth; in the fellowship of our fellow pilgrims helping one another in the heat of the tour; and in the courage of the Christian Arab minority in Bethlehem.

Here is another of those both/and situations which help us to see both sides of the truth.

Having found our roots in this tense land, holy for different groups for such different and often conflicting reasons, can we dare to raise the tensions that already exist by encouraging celebrations here and else-where in the year 2000?

The answer again is 'Yes and no'. Yes, we have a right and a privilege to claim our roots in this soil. It is the place in which the Saviour was born, lived, died and rose again. Christ has a rightful place in this land. It cannot be denied or ignored. Yes, we also have a duty to our brothers and sisters in Nazareth, Bethlehem and Jerusalem to help them celebrate this part of their history and ours. Their numbers are in decline, mostly through emigration to places of greater opportunity for their children, and they need our support and our care. Many depend on the visits of pilgrims for their livelihood and are finding the present restrictions crippling. They need both the pilgrim and the tourist. Yes, for our own sake we also need to find our roots in this land to proclaim the truth that Christianity is an historical religion where Jesus was real, and God was made known to us through a particular person, at a particular time, and in a particular place.

But no, we must exercise our rights and our duties with care and sensitivity. We pilgrims must not take possession of the space belonging to others. We must respect the local people who live on the land, especially the Christian remnant. We must not act with arrogance towards our neighbours, even those who might threaten us by their dominance.

A number of churches have plans for the improvement of Manger Square at Bethlehem as a sign of the importance of the year AD 2000. If these programmes are carried out cooperatively and with sensitivity, then they will be a witness to the Prince of Peace, born at Bethlehem. If not, they will only add to the tension and be a cause of dismay to those who have over many centuries hallowed the Church of the Nativity with their prayers and their purse.

From the roots of the stem of Jesse let the branches of peace and proclamation shoot forth. Then we will have discovered why the date is significant, and how people and places have been part of the wonderful story of the birth of the Saviour, not only of the people of that soil and time, but of those from all the nations of the world.

3

HOLDING HANDS
AT PRAYER

A number of times in the previous chapter I have referred to pilgrims at prayer, and indicated that prayer brought us directly into the presence of God. We can visit places which connect us to our historical roots, and thereby feel close to God. God's presence can also be revealed to us, wherever we are in the world, through prayer. In this chapter I will explore what prayer is, why we pray, how we pray 'in Christ', and how prayer forms part of our relationship with God. Later I will look at the various ingredients that make up prayer – such as acknowledgement, adoration, confession, thanksgiving, offering, supplication and intercession. I conclude the chapter with a focus on the Lord's Prayer, which is a summary of all prayerful activity, making it a point of continuity with the past, the present and the future for all Christian people.

In the year 2000 Christians are encouraged not only to witness to the Faith which traces its roots back through those 2000 years, but also to recognize their present relationship with God. God is as active in shaping the world today as in all previous times from the Creation onwards. God the Holy Spirit – or, as this can also be expressed, 'the Spirit of Jesus Christ' – is not limited by boundaries of place or time. The Spirit therefore keeps us in the presence of God wherever we are and in whatever generation we have life. 'Closer than breathing' is the description often used for the Spirit's presence. This takes up the root meaning of the word in both of the original languages of the Scriptures – *ruach* in Hebrew and *pneuma* in Greek. In English we need a range of words to gain a full picture of the meaning of the one word 'spirit': wind, breath, forceful power, the essence of life. You can see how hard it is to convey the double meaning of Genesis 2:7:

> then the Lord God formed man [*adam*] from the dust of the ground [*adamah*],
> and breathed into his nostrils the breath [*ruach*] of life;
> and the man became a living being.

The verse indicates that the author saw God as giving to humanity the life-giving capacity to breathe and at the same time God gave humanity the 'spirit'– the Divine quality of being fully alive and receptive to the presence of God. It is in prayer that we experience for ourselves this double sense of being alive through God's creativity and of being capable of linking our spirits with the Spirit of God. It is important for Christians to witness to this gift of God as we enter the third millennium, and make prayer part of our 'Worship 2000' celebrations.

WHAT IS PRAYER?

Many people ask, 'What is prayer?' Here is a brief definition which should help to clarify our response to such a question: *Prayer is the human activity which responds to the work of the Holy Spirit within us, and enables us to enter into a relationship with God through a dialogue of acknowledgement and the interchange of wills.*

Prayer is a human activity which is in response to the initiative of God. Humans can pray because God has breathed such a spirit of prayer into our human body. None of us in our own power can approach God in prayer. We cannot take the initiative in the relationship with God, for that would be to reverse the God/human roles. Fortunately for us all, God has already taken that initiative, and given us the power to pray. Paul's Epistle to the Church at Rome (8:26–27) tells us that the Holy Spirit 'helps us in our weakness' when it comes to praying, and prays in and through us:

> Likewise the Spirit helps us in our weakness; for we do not know how to pray as we ought, but that very Spirit intercedes with sighs too deep for words. And God, who searches the heart, knows what is the mind of the Spirit, because the Spirit intercedes for the saints according to the will of God.

Through prayer we enter into a relationship with God in an intimate, contemporary and personal way. Many people find it helpful to shape the 'personal' side of God by their picture of Jesus. For them prayer becomes a 'conversation with Christ'. Obviously the writer of the Epistle to the Hebrews (4:14–15) had such an experience in mind when he wrote:

> Since we have a great high priest who has passed through the heavens, Jesus the Son of God ... let us therefore approach the throne of grace with boldness, so that we may receive mercy and find grace to help in time of need.

Knowing Jesus, now ascended into the unity of the Godhead, we are able to find the courage and the familiarity (the family links) to pray 'with boldness'. Such an attitude is not one of arrogance but one of humble acknowledgement that we are privileged to enter into such a relationship with God.

The Epistle to the Hebrews contains many passages which encourage Christians to approach God in prayer. We are right to retain a sense of awe in the presence of God, but this is not a sense of overwhelming fear. The writer of the Epistle draws our attention to the fact that we can picture Jesus praying for us. He 'is always able to save [maybe with the sense of 'keep safe'] those who approach God through him, since he always lives to make intercession for them' (Hebrews 7:25). This is very like hearing someone say to us, 'I will keep you in my prayers.' We feel supported by this and are given new strength to face the issues before us.

Such prayer acknowledges the privilege of being able to enter directly into the presence of God, there to acknowledge God's goodness, love and care for us and all the created order. In such a way we affirm who God is and what God does. In prayer the flow of thoughts and words are not all one way. We not only address God with words of affection and worship, but also listen to God's acknowledgement of us. We find our true selves in the presence of this loving God, and this empowers us to offer our lives to achieve the purposes that God has for Creation. The dialogue is a sign of the intimacy of the relationship built up in prayer. It leads into the meeting of minds about the right thing to do for ourselves and for all those we touch and influence. Such prayer becomes an interchange of wills. Each knows the other so well that they can see what the other wants and how that might be achieved.

All this moves us a long way from seeing prayer as a shopping list of requests, similar to that which little children might bring to parents –

'gi'me' prayers, as some have called them. It is not surprising that society views such prayers as magical if answered, or as denying the existence of God if they are not. One of the useful aspects of celebrating the year 2000 is that we can look back over the 2000 years and find inspiration in the teaching of the great leaders in prayer, who are to be found among all Christian traditions in every century. They can help us to see that the goal of prayer is the full maturity of the relationship with God. Some have called this 'mystical union' with God. For me the best term to use is 'a union of heart and mind with the God who is revealed for us in Jesus Christ'. In this way all prayer is linked with Christ's prayer, and as we live in Christ so we also pray in Christ. This concept leads to a further response to the question, What is prayer? We can add to our answer this further definition: *Prayer is the activity of joining ourselves with the Ascended Christ in the inauguration of the rule of God, in earth as in heaven.*

WHY PRAY?

We pray because prayer is a joyful activity which allows us as human beings to exercise the Divine Spirit breathed into us. Praying is a very satisfying activity because it fulfils the height of human potential; it demonstrates our full humanity; it allows us to participate in the future of the world; and it keeps us constantly in touch with God. It is true that Christians feel an obligation to pray. It is the Christian response to God's call to enter into and sustain the relationship with God. So we can affirm:

It is our duty and our joy, always and everywhere,
to offer prayer and adoration to God.

We also pray because as partners of Christ we join Christ in bringing wholeness to the Universe. We add our spiritual energy and the obedience of our human response to that of Christ, empowering the world to fulfil its destiny of true harmony and wholeness – the *shalom* of God. Some people find it hard to see how God would want them in such a partnership. They ask: 'What difference does it make to the outcome that I pray?' Surprisingly, the answer seems to be that God wishes such a partnership, and each partner does make a difference. This does not deny the power of God. It is obvious that God *could* do anything without us. However, the Scriptures tell us that God has chosen to work *with* us. Humanity is called to be a partner with God in bringing the world to wholeness. Those engaged in farming or who gain their livelihood from the land will be very aware that they work in partnership with the Creator. Only cooperation will achieve the full potential of the land. In a similar way it is possible for us to imagine the role that we have as Christians at prayer in achieving wholeness and harmony for all of Creation.

I find it ludicrous to listen to people at prayer drawing God's attention to some issues. This seems to imply that God either does not know, or does not care enough, about what is going on in God's world. Words such as 'God, we want you to know that John is in hospital with a broken leg' or 'God, remember Jean, who is lonely at this time' seem to confuse God's role and ours. God knows already about John and Jean, and Christ is already at prayer for them, so the words in our prayers must reflect this reality. More appropriate words in these situations might be:

> God of caring love, continue to support John as his broken leg heals. Grant him patience and a relaxed body even in its pain, so that your healing power is at work in him. Help us to be sensitive to his needs as we support him too.
>
> We pray also for Jean, loved as part of your family in Christ. Help her to be aware of your presence with her in her times of loneliness, and inspire those who reach out to her to know how to respond to her needs. This prayer we make with Christ, and in his name. Amen.

The exact words of a prayer are not the essentials in praying, but we do need to make certain that they reflect a theology of God which makes sense to us, and does not reduce God to a dictator or a casino operator, handing out favours to the lucky ones.

WHO PRAYS?

As we take up our responsibilities to pray, we can find encouragement in knowing not only that Christ already prays with us and for us, but also that Christians pray in the company of the whole Christian community – the Universal Church. The Spirit of Christ dwells within this community and each member of it. This makes prayer a corporate activity and each member of the Church shares in this combined task. This allows us to free ourselves from feeling that it is our task, and our task alone, to pray for everything and everybody. On the other hand, we must take our proper share of the work. As in all team situations, the work of each member is vital to the achievement of the whole. In the work of prayer the Universal Church complements and completes the work of each part. Prayer weaves a pattern of wholeness into the praise and petition of the total Christian community. In this way strong links are forged between different parts of the One Church through prayer. Those suffering persecution are supported by those with more relative peace. Those who are dispirited because of lack of any response to the Gospel in their area are upheld by the prayers of the many who are finding new hope and faith in the Gospel in another area. In the next chapter, 'Holding Hands across the Globe', we will look more closely at this interdependence in prayer, but it should be noted here that in the year 2000 there will be a good opportunity for each part of the Universal Church to support the others through prayer.

PRAYER AS RELATIONSHIP

The year 2000 sees a world longing for deeper relationships within families, communities and within the global village. To have a relationship with God helps us to develop more mature relationships with one another. Prayer is one of the key ways of entering and sustaining our relationship with God. When we compare the ways in which we maintain our human relationships with our actions in prayer which enhance our relationship with God, the following points can be noted:

- Prayer helps us to acknowledge who we are and what we mean to God. In turn we find ourselves acknowledged by God as important to the relationship. In this way we build up a mutual feeling of love and respect.
- Prayer allows us to express such feelings in words of adoration, praise, value and delight to be in each other's company.
- When something has occurred to damage the relationship, in prayer we can express sorrow and repentance, and know again from God that, through the Cross, Christ has taken the initiative to bear the pain of the breakdown, and with love and forgiveness has restored the relationship.
- Prayer allows us to express our words of thanks for all that has enhanced the relationship, both in the past and in the present. This will include thanksgiving for the initiatives that God has taken on our behalf – our creation, our forgiveness, our renewal, our empowerment through the Holy Spirit. In turn God will offer thanks for our willingness to share in the partnership with adoration and obedience.

41

- Prayer helps us to declare our desire to find the best course of action for the future, and to seek strength to implement the mutually decided will.
- Prayer is the channel for the empowerment of the Holy Spirit and the sign of our acceptance of this for our lives. Through it we are in a position to fulfil the goals that have been set.
- Because our relationship with God always affects those around us, we naturally want to share with God our love and concern for those whose lives touch ours. Prayer allows us to express such concern and to reaffirm that God already has these people close to the heart.
- Prayer within such a relationship will not be based on words alone, but will employ all the usual means of communication – emotions, silence, 'touch' and reflective listening.

When Christians are faithful in developing such relationships with God through prayer, then their lives reach such a measure of maturity that it embraces their relationships with everyone around them. So we can be in a better position to respond to the issues that many are raising at the start of the new millennium. Most people want there to be a reduction in the number of suicides; less physical and emotional abuse; a reversal of the destruction of the value placed on people; less strife and killing within communities; and an end to war between communities. The Christian has a positive response to offer to these cries. The development of relationships through the practice of prayer is part of the Good News they share with the world.

PRAYER AS ACKNOWLEDGEMENT

Let us make a fuller examination of the issues behind a suicide. Suicide, particularly among younger people, normally so full of positive attitudes to life, is one of the saddest phenomena of the late twentieth century. Clearly, some young people feel that they are of such little value that there is no loss, and maybe even a gain, in taking their own lives. This lack of value is an offshoot of the attitudes of a society in which success is said to come by luck, status through money, position by successful moves in a competitive world, and human life is able to be discarded like material goods in a throw-away society. One of the key ways by which we develop value as human beings is by the affirmation of worth that is expressed in a true relationship. We need to hear such words as: 'I value your place in the family; I value your friendship in our relationship; I value your contribution to the future of our society.'

In prayer our acknowledgement of God is returned in full measure by God's acknowledgement of us: 'You are my beloved child; you are my partner in working for the future; you are valued as a unique part of my Creation; you are therefore valued for who you are even more than for what you can do.' Current discussions about allowing euthanasia for the chronically sick or the aged person, who has lost rational sensitivities or bodily functions, also devalues human life *for its own sake*, focusing instead on the so-called usefulness or otherwise of that life. Even the value of the life of the sick person in serious pain is able to be enhanced by current techniques which still allow maximum awareness consistent with reduction in pain. This is the aim of the Hospice Movement worldwide. In such a state they are still able to participate in prayer – even if only for fleeting moments of full consciousness – and thus affirm their value through their relationship with God, and with those they love and pray for. Some other people may formulate the words for them, but the 'Amen' will be theirs, full of faith and affirmation.

Suicide is sometimes the final outcome of abuse, and in such situations Christians have the gift of God's forgiveness to offer. The forgiveness offered is that which comes from God to heal the sense of guilt which the abused carry, even when no fault would be accorded by others to that person. The sense of guilt can often only be removed from their spirit by such a powerful symbol as the Cross – the place where Jesus, without guilt, carried the guilt and burden of humanity's sin. Observing that such forgiveness is a generous gift from God, the abused receive it gladly and rejoice in its freedom and release. However, some struggle with the perceived obligation that they must at the same time forgive their abusers. Sometimes such people are known to those they abuse from a relationship within the circle of family or friends. Prayer and counsel should help to clarify how and when such forgiveness is possible. For the abuser repentance is part of the process, and that takes time and true humility, and this is not part of the responsibility of the abused. The forgiveness of God to the abused often has to be received in its own right and absorbed with patience before any thoughts are addressed about how to forgive those who caused the wrong. For such abused people the prayer of acknowledgement is vital for the trust it shows in God and the value that is returned to the worshipper by God. Through such prayer self-esteem, lost through abuse, is built up again.

PRAYER AS ADORATION

Our adoration of God in prayer helps us to regain our sense of trust in the purpose of God for all of the created order and for ourselves as part of it. By praising God in prayer we affirm who God is for us, and what are the qualities that God possesses. Such adoration helps us to see the proper place for humanity in the relationship with God. If the places are reversed, humankind starts to express an arrogance and a dominance which leads to the oppression of others. Then humanity falsely believes that it is in a position of supreme authority and power, and human beings can take control of others and of all the created order. In such an upside-down world supreme power would lie in the hands of those who thought that they were accountable to no one – on earth or heaven. Such ideas are highly dangerous and lead to oppression and violence towards others. The twentieth century has seen more than enough dictators and wars to fill a whole millennium, and many have a strong desire to rid the world of such people as the new century begins. Prayer is an important antidote to the poison of oppression, as long as no one believes that they can borrow God's power and authority and use it to overpower others. Only a distorted view of God would allow a person at prayer to twist its use for such a purpose. History will warn us of the possibility and should prevent us from such corruption.

PRAYER AS CONFESSION

The Reconciliation and Justice Commission in the Republic of South Africa shows a mighty attempt by a Christian nation to put prayers of confession and forgiveness into action. Desmond Tutu and other Christian prophets and martyrs have played a leading role in creating this Commission and making it work so successfully. The Commission's policy has given citizens an opportunity to admit their wrongdoing, show genuine repentance and seek forgiveness from the whole community through the Commission. Such work has begun to release the nation from hidden and suppressed guilt, unspoken sorrow, and so fear of the possibility of a return to the cycle of violence. Within a nation the proposals for such a commission could only have been formulated by those who had examined their own consciences in prayers of confession. Only when we have come to terms with the fact that we are all sinners, guilty of destroying by some action our relationship with God and one another, are we in a position to accept the admission of another person of their sin, and still offer them the opportunity of forgiveness from God and then from ourselves. On the other hand, the self-righteous – those who say that they have no sin – are only too quick to condemn others and exact a penalty to hurt the sinner, leaving a community broken and angry. The forgiven sinner, however, will be more ready to admit their own faults and thus be able to listen to the words of confession from another, allowing God to forgive them, and in turn offering to restore the relationship.

In prayer the purpose of confession is always the restoration of the relationship and renewed unity and mutuality. Its aim is reconciliation. The essential step in reaching this goal is a full admission of responsibility for the wrong and a serious attempt to rectify the hurt. Knowing the promise of forgiveness is a strong encouragement to the one who prays words of confession. Aware that we will be treated with justice and love, we are more ready to admit our wrongdoing and seek the power to renew our lives in righteousness. We will know that the act of forgiveness can only be granted at a cost to the one who is forgiving.

In the year 2000 we will all need to seek reconciliation and renewal. It is good to see the attempts in many countries to express sorrow for past injustices and to take actions leading to reconciliation. Many indigenous peoples, who have been deprived of their heritage of land, are hearing with joy the representatives of the community making confession for the injustices done and seeking to heal the hurts. In turn the people of the land need to respond to such confession with forgiveness, which is always costly for them. They cannot demand compensation to an equal extent to the deprivation. Otherwise it is only an act of 'tit for tat' contract and not forgiveness at all. The present-day participants are not those who caused or received the hurt, and are therefore not in a position to make total remedy for the faults. The present generation can all, on the other hand, accept responsibility for reconciliation, and by confession and forgiveness, by tokens of justice and mutual care, reach a new unity in creating a new future for the whole nation. Care must be taken to see that the motive of greed is excluded and any settlements do not lead to the pain of jealousy and further rivalry.

The year 2000 is also an opportunity for communities to work to heal the hurts of the past which are causing the violence of the present. The 'peace process' can only proceed on a firm footing when communities are ready to acknowledge that everyone to a greater or lesser extent has contributed to these divisions. This acknowledgement can lead to an act of mutual confession and mutual forgiveness under God. Out of such seeds of honesty and reconciliation peace is born for the future. There is no doubt that this will be the hope of many Christians and others in Bourgainville, Northern Ireland, Rwanda, Israel, South Africa and, on a smaller scale, within divided local communities in so many different parts of the globe.

Such acts of reconciliation through prayer can form part of the national and local celebrations for the year 2000, and examples of suitable prayers will be found in Chapters 7 and 8 of this book. What is true for communities is also true for families and between individuals. It is a sign of deep wisdom in the Church that in nearly all acts of worship an opportunity for a time of confession and forgiveness is given. This is not included to pile on the pressure for worshippers to feel guilty, but so that no person is left without the opportunity to hear the words of absolution and forgiveness to release them from their guilt. No one should depart a service of Christian worship still carrying a burden of guilt. Often we need to hear that God promises us forgiveness before we have the courage to ask forgiveness from the human person we have hurt or from whom we are estranged. If God can forgive us, then we have the strength to ask our neighbour to forgive us too. The possibility of forgiveness and the promise of God's forgiveness are incentives for Christians to offer the Good News of reconciliation to those in their community. There will be rejoicing across the globe whenever the Christian community by action and example offers and receives this ministry of reconciliation, and both individuals and sections of society hear the powerful words: 'You are forgiven. Be at peace.'

PRAYER AS THANKSGIVING

Such rejoicing will lead to acts of joyful thanksgiving. Gratitude to God will not only be for the gift of forgiveness and the reconciliation which follows, but for all the wonders of God's love and of God's Creation. Thanksgiving in prayer restores a sense of perspective in our lives. When the desire and wish-list for more than the essentials recedes further and further away, and when we discover that the more we have the more we want, it is acts of thanksgiving that restore our sense of balance. Without such prayers, depression and desperation can often set in. The year 2000 will give us a wonderful opportunity to consider the present in the light of what has been given to us rather than in the darkness of what we lack. Anxiety about possessions destroys rich and poor alike. The circumstances are very different but the principle is the same. Conversely, thanksgiving enriches the spirit of both poor and rich alike. In thanksgiving we acknowledge that all life is a gift, and the greatest gift is God's love – that is, God's assurance and God's spirit of courage and maturity which helps us respond to all the situations of life.

In giving thanks to God we also offer our thanks for the human agents of such gifts. In the year 2000 we will give thanks for the inheritance that past generations have built up for us. As we do so we will realize that we too are only stewards for our time. We are to enjoy what we have been given, and to be responsible for passing on, with the additions we have made, this heritage to generations yet to be born. We will learn in this way to have a greater respect for the past, to be more accountable to the future, and to be wiser for the present. Such prayers of thanksgiving should help us with the vital issues of conservation in our communities. Of course, we are well aware that we cannot preserve the past as if we were living in those days. We can only take care of the treasures of the past in the context of the present, so that the future will be able to enjoy what has been bequeathed to them. We are called to be managers of sustainable use. As such we need great wisdom to decide how to preserve without storing life as if we were in a museum. Those in charge of museums have themselves changed the way they are run. Nowadays the object is to inform as well as collect, to relate the past to the present, to allow the past to give a perspective on the present, and to gather the treasures of the current generation for the delight of future ones. By their prayers of thanksgiving Christians are assisting the community in considering how the past can be part of today's living, and how the gifts of the present should be used to enhance the world of tomorrow as well as today.

PRAYER AS OFFERING

The year 2000 is the opportunity to consider our actions for the future. Christians seek to be partners with God in discerning the best courses of action to take, and in discovering the means to put them into practice. Our aim is a 'mutuality of wills'. Ten years ago in New Zealand a group of Christian leaders were guided in prayer to propose a consultation for leaders in the community to enable them to discover a vision for the coming decade. The year 1990 was the one hundred and fiftieth anniversary of the nation as well as the beginning of a decade, and this added impetus to the plan. The event was called '*Te Ara Tika* / The Way Ahead', using the two official languages of the country. The participants were encouraged by the interchange of ideas in the context of worship and prayer. They gathered mutual strength through cooperation to tackle the difficult issues that faced the nation at that time. The goodwill engendered was impressive and led to positive initiatives in many fields. Many at the consultation found it was helpful to be able to identify other Christian people (from different church communities) who were in key positions within their society, and to see how the debates were supported by expertise, reflection and prayer. No one Christian response was identified on many issues, but it was clear what Christian principles lay behind the various proposals. There was a series of cooperative debates about issues concerning methods of governance, education, health, welfare, economics and cultural mutuality. The spirit of the debate was one of discernment, not competition; for the good of the *polis*,[1] not politics; of building up, not tearing down. The consultation did find some 'ways ahead' and concluded with an act of thanksgiving and dedication, when those attending offered their skills and wills to try to do what was right, true, just and wise for all the members of our society.

I share this experience in this book about worship in the year 2000 in the hope that around the globe Christians in the various nations will seriously consider a parallel event in their communities as a way of saying to God: 'Your will be done.' As Christians we do not hold to a doctrine which declares that God has set down the future path for us in detail so that we can sit back and simply allow God's plan for the future to unfold. We do believe that God has the future held securely for us and has set out the directions that we should follow. However, the details of implementation and decision-making are our responsibility *with* God, as part of the mutual partnership into which we are called. Human beings are part of the struggle to discern the truth, to establish justice, to maintain mutual care, and to enhance the lives of all within society. In some Christian communities the clergy alone are assigned the role of being the voice of prophetic Christian teaching, whereas the expertise in most areas lies in the hands of the laity. There seem to be few opportunities for those who are wise in Christian principles to meet with those who are experienced and equipped to implement those principles in the various fields of community endeavour. The clergy/laity divide is a major hindrance at this point. Both can also retreat into a heresy of predetermination when faced with difficulties. They hope that God can fix the problems that people have created. Clergy and laity need to cooperate to discern the possibility for future plans and together assist the community to make the choice of the ones most suitable. Then our prayers will be informed by research and expertise, and community knowledge will grow wise from reflective prayer.

SUPPLICATION

Future plans, however wise they are, will not create a new future without the courage, skill and strength that are the gifts of the Spirit of God. As we face the future in the year 2000 we will make supplication in prayer for such gifts for ourselves and for our communities. To pray in this way is not a sign of weakness but a sign that we are strong and confident enough to ask for help. Christians will unite in prayer at the beginning of the new millennium to seek help to fulfil the dreams of God and themselves for a new world, which builds on the old but corrects its mistakes and imbalances. The prophets of doom are no longer the priests but the scientists. They warn us of global warming, mutation of viruses that cause disease, over-population, famine and the outcomes of arrogant human experimentation. The voice of the economist is added to warn of hell in the form of the collapse of global finance markets, currency corruption, unemployment and the devaluation of labour and property. The voice of the conservationists warns us of the collapse of the Creation itself with the elimination of species, the acid wasting of forests, the submerging of the low-lying islands in the oceans, and the depletion of the ozone layer. Such warnings are realistic, but they lack the prophetic word of hope that God is ready to give us the Spirit to enable us with new strength to tackle the issues and find a new way of positive living. In our prayers, repentance and supplication will join hands and new energy and determination will replace depression. Improvement will not happen unless we believe that there is something that can be done to change the situation and that our efforts can create new possibilities. As we enter the new millennium Christians can witness to the fact that active prayer can overcome the enemies of doom and despair with the gifts of hope and faith.

INTERCESSION

It is right that we should begin by praying for ourselves so that we can become filled with new hope and strength. Once our spirits have been built up we can reach out our hands to others to help everyone gain a new sense of confidence and accountability. So we will intercede for others. In such prayers we will become intertwined with the intercessions of God and the saints – the faithful of all generations. We will join our energy and love with the Divine energy and love to bring healing, wholeness and justice to the world. The miracle of prayer is that people find that they are upheld in the corporate action of supportive love so that they have the strength to face the situation that is before them. God has taken the initiative to give us such love, and has told us clearly that there is nothing that can separate such love from us – no disaster of death or life, no oppression of the world as it is or as it might be, no failure or threat from Creation, that can separate us from the love and care of God. With such a promise of comfort to uphold us, we can sail through the storms, face the future and still hold our heads up high in confident trust. Too often we turn to prayer as an easy way out of the situation, asking God to remove the danger and free us from the responsibility of dealing with it. It is hard to learn the lesson of Gethsemane, where even Jesus had to affirm again that the cup of suffering must be drunk, for it cannot be removed without the destruction of all human responsibility and freedom.

Prayers of intercession are never easy or comfortable. They always force us to face the reality for others that only love is victorious, and joy is in resurrection and recovery, not in the avoidance of the crucial issue. This is why Christians at the end of their prayers of intercession often feel exhausted. As we commit ourselves to prayer at the beginning of the millennium we should be equally realistic about the cost as well as the reward of prayer. We share in the joy of Christ at seeing the courage and hope that prayer brings about, but we also know how painful it is as we struggle with our feelings of hopelessness and helplessness.

In the Introduction the question was raised: *Can Christ, who intercedes for us, understand the experiences behind our prayers now that life is so different at the beginning of a new millennium?* In this chapter we have seen that Christians do not pray for Christ to produce some magic to solve our technical problems. We pray that Christ will share with us the spirit of human maturity which gives us, as a local or world community, the wisdom, determination and courage to work out the solutions to our problems. Such solutions will always put people first and material comfort and profit in second place. Mindful of this, we can see that it is the humanity of Christ rather than the generation, gender, culture or race that gives Christ the right to be our companion in prayer. In our prayers for peace, for example, we are seeking to bring the spirit of harmony, respect, cooperation, forgiveness and restraint to those who must make decisions about how to live alongside their neighbours. The Scriptures (cf. Galatians 5:22–23) see these qualities as the gifts of the Spirit of Christ, and these are the qualities that we observe in Jesus Christ during his years of ministry. As we pray for peace we ask that men and women may have the courage to overcome the divisions of the past and present, strengthened by the hope that hurts can be healed and the future holds out possibilities for a change in human attitudes and behaviour. The Gospel of Jesus Christ is founded on this hope for humanity. The technical details of living may have changed, but the fundamental principles of living have not changed. The pace of life has accelerated but the true direction for life remains static. Humans still search for maturity, for the ability to live with God, to live in harmony with ourselves and those who live alongside us. Jesus Christ has shown that he understands this search and upholds us in prayer as we undertake our journey from birth to death and resurrection.

The Ascension doctrine tells us that the experience of being human is firmly within the heart of God, and in our prayers we can be certain that God does understand 'from the inside'. The Godhead holds together in perfect unity the knowledge of the created order with the experience itself of being part of that order as a human being. There can be no situation which is outside the understanding of God.

THE LORD'S PRAYER

Some things can be said to be true for all time – eternal truths that are treasured by each generation and passed on from one to the next. Sometimes these truths are conveyed in the form of proverbs. One example which is well known is 'The early bird catches the worm', meaning that the person who takes the initiative receives their reward. Other truths have been passed on in the words of prayers. For Christians the Lord's Prayer is the best example. Christ taught this prayer to his disciples in response to a request from them to 'teach us how to pray'. A form of the prayer is recorded in the Gospels of Matthew (6:9–13) and Luke (11:2–4). The several phrases of the Lord's Prayer mirror the main aspects of prayer that we have examined in this chapter. This becomes obvious when the prayer is set out in columns comparing each heading with phrases of the Lord's Prayer put into contemporary wording:

Prayer as relationship.	*Our heavenly Father,*
Prayer as acknowledgement and adoration.	*we praise and honour you.*
Prayer as the mutuality of wills.	*May your rule extend, and your will be done in the world as it is fulfilled in heaven.*
Prayer as supplication for ourselves and intercession for others.	*Give us this day sufficient rations to meet our daily needs.*
Prayer as confession.	*Forgive us our wrongdoing, as we forgive those who have hurt us.*
Prayer for strength and protection.	*Do not bring us to the time of severe testing (when we could not cope), but rescue us from evil.*

In the opening line of the prayer Jesus taught his disciples to address God in the most intimate child-to-parent language possible. The term Abba is one of endearment and trust, and its use enhances our relationship with God. Entering into such a relationship helps us to understand the mind of God, and so we pray that our living may be shaped by the coming of the rule of God, by restraining our requests to ask only for the practical necessities of life, by the promise to forgive others as we ask God to forgive us, and by the confidence that God will give us the strength to cope with our times of trial, but not ask us to face overwhelming forces of evil. When we make this prayer we do so both for our own selves and for those for whom we want to pray. We want them to enter into such a wonderful relationship and to receive the gifts they need for full living in God's Kingdom.

This prayer embodies eternal truths that have applied in the past, are current for the present, and will operate fully in the future. At the turn of the first millennium there was much talk of 'end times', just as there had been after Jesus' ascension. People then expected God to inaugurate a dramatic 'new order of existence'. As we have seen, the events of Jesus' incarnation, death, resurrection and ascension did begin a new period of history. Our celebrations for the year 2000 bear witness to this. But these events are within time, not beyond time, and create new goals and power for human living, not a totally new order of existence where time and power are transformed by glory. We should approach the words of the

Lord's Prayer with the both/and principle. It is a prayer both for our times and for the end times, when all things are transformed into a new type of existence. The latter is called an 'eschatological' interpretation, and the prayer can be used as a petition and promise of the 'final age of God'. Then the rule of God will be brought to perfection for us and for the whole of Creation. The bread for today is a foretaste of the final banquet when all people will be gathered to celebrate the full disclosure (*parousia*) of the victory of Christ. The debts that will be forgiven then will signal the settling of the final accounts to accumulate the treasures of Christ. Then the time of trial and testing will be the final agony and struggle as the victory of justice, righteousness and peace is won, and all evil is overcome and eliminated.

The truth has to be that this prayer is continuously applicable to the now and to the future. We will use it for today as well as for the final day, for realistically both are intertwined and equal in the power of God.

At the end of the prayer as recorded in the Gospel of Matthew some early scribes, when copying the words, added an ascription of praise to the text as an excited response. This evidence would point to the widespread use of the prayer in the Early Church and to the inclusion in the liturgy of such words of affirmation:

For you, O God, rule and reign with power and glory,
now and for the ages to come. Amen, true it is, and true may it be.

We too will want to add such words of praise and affirmation to a prayer which sums up so beautifully all the thoughts and words that we want to share with God.

Familiarity is both a plus and a minus for the use of this prayer in public worship. It allows all those using it to feel in touch with the prayers of Christ's disciples down the ages and across the globe in this generation. It also recalls all the intimate times in the past when we have experienced God as understanding and responding to our supplications. The Lord's Prayer allows words from the depth of our memory to articulate our thoughts, and this helps us to pray even when we struggle to formulate our needs into phrases. On the other hand, its very familiarity can mean that we pass the prayer over our lips without it passing through our minds. When that happens we come to the end of the prayer hardly knowing what we have said. The speed with which it is repeated often causes the hiatus between the lips and the mind.

I believe the Lord's Prayer – as the universal prayer among all Christian communities – should be used as part of our celebrations for 'Worship 2000', but special care should be employed in the way this is done. The words should be expressed in the variety of languages spoken by the assembled people, and if appropriate, sung to music. This allows the words more time to penetrate into the conscious mind. Where this is not suitable, the old custom of repeating the prayer line by line after the leader might prove useful. As with the good wine of the Gospel, our lips should be given ample time to savour the richness of this beautiful and powerful prayer.

SUMMARY

All types of prayer will form a central position in the work of Christians in the year 2000. It will be their offering of thanksgiving, their words of dedication and commitment, their pleas for help to be proper partners of Christ in the implementation of the Kingdom. Prayer will express their cries for strength and protection to overcome the evil that is so obvious in our 'end times'.

As we hold our hands together in prayer we will be conscious of the great company of saints in Christ who, through the generations and across the globe, are holding our hands in unity and love.

4

HOLDING HANDS
ACROSS THE GLOBE

From its roots in Nazareth, Bethlehem and Jerusalem a faith in Jesus as Christ and Lord spread rapidly over the boundaries of nations, until it stretched to the limits of the travelled world. The presence of Christ through prayer and sacrament made such an expansion possible, and the world of the first century seemed eager for a religion which engaged heart and mind, and provided a new moral and ethical code for living, both individually and collectively.

MANY CULTURES IN THE PENTECOST CROWD

Luke, writing in the Acts of the Apostles, maps out this expansion in the experience of the pilgrims gathered at Jerusalem for Pentecost. In Acts 2:8–11 he pictures the presence of people from many cultures in the crowd on the day of the revelation of the Holy Spirit to the disciples. These pilgrims ask:

> How is it that we hear, each of us, in our own native language? Parthians, Medes, Elamites, and residents of Mesopotamia, Judea and Cappodocia, Pontus and Asia, Phrygia and Pamphylia, Egypt and the parts of Libya belonging to Cyrene, and visitors from Rome, both Jews and proselytes, Cretans and Arabs, in our own languages we hear them speaking about God's deeds of power.

Such a list of names has always been a test of the ability of the reader of Scripture. Even to pronounce the names correctly was a success, never mind having any idea of the geographical location of these names! Fortunately some modern translations of the Bible[1] have included maps on which these names are inserted. In summary, we can see that the first four names – Parthia, Media, Elam and Mesopotamia – are the nations and empires of the East, lying beyond the rivers Euphrates and Tigris towards the Caspian Sea. These territories are now part of the 'Arab World' – Iran, Iraq and Syria. The second group of names represents the north, towards the Black Sea, and Pontus and Cappadocia are now within the area of Turkey. Also within modern Turkey but further west is the group Asia, Phrygia and Pamphylia. This reference is not to the 'Asia' we think of now, but 'Asia Minor', the lands where St Paul travelled a number of times to strengthen the newly planted churches of the first century. One of its key cities was Ephesus on the coast, and another was Pisidan Antioch in the centre of the territory.

Surprisingly, in Luke's description of Pentecost there is no mention of the people of the Greek peninsula. Common (*Koine*) Greek was widely spoken as a language for trade purposes, and it became a means of international communication for the early Christians. It was the chosen language of the authors of the various parts of the New Testament. In the record of Acts it is not until chapter 16 that we hear of Paul having a vision of a man from Macedonia, calling him to travel west, and the movement towards the Greek people began.

The southern regions of the known world are represented in Luke's list by Egypt and Cyrene, key centres in North Africa. This became a fruitful area of Christian mission and was later the home of a number of Early Church theologians such as Origen, Tertullian and Cyprian, and was the birthplace of Augustine of Hippo. The next and the most distant place named in this passage was seen in those times as the centre of the world – the city of Rome, the heart of the Empire. It was at least 2300 kilometres in a direct line from Jerusalem, and to get there involved a long journey by sea across the Mediterranean in which the isle of Crete was about the half-way point. We know from the record of Paul's journey in the closing chapters of Acts that this was a rough, dangerous crossing in the winter months. When he finally reached Rome in the spring, Paul was welcomed by 'believers' (Acts 28:14), so the faith in Jesus Christ had reached the city long before he did.

The last area mentioned as having representatives at Pentecost was Arabia. This territory stretched through the desert lands to the south-east of Judea, eventually reaching the Indian Ocean. These pilgrims would have come nearly as far as those who crossed the seas from Rome, but their travels were over seas of sand from the trading ports of the Persian Gulf. Now this territory belongs to Saudi Arabia and its Gulf State neighbours.

Right at the outset of the expansion of the Gospel we see people from north, south, east and west holding hands across the globe in mutual understanding and support. Luke makes it clear that the message of the Gospel was understood 'in the language of the people' from near and far. The Good News made sense in many different cultures, for language preserves culture. From the outset Christianity would be a religion for all nations. This passage in Acts 2 points to the reversal of the experience of the people at Babel in Genesis 11:1–9. There the people are said to have been punished for their arrogance in erecting a tower to proclaim their superiority to everyone, including God. Their failure to acknowledge the priority of God splits them apart and they become confused and disunited in communication. At God's initiative, at the coming of the Spirit, the work of unity and understanding is re-established. The scene is set for a Church which united the people of the world in one faith and one purpose.

THE WORLD IN WHICH WE LIVE

The world in which this first generation of Christian people lived had some features which have remarkable similarities to those of our own day.

Transportation was becoming easier and people were able to move from place to place in pursuit of work and new prospects. There was an international work-force, created partly by commercial opportunity and partly by the movement of slaves to provide labour for the rich, both in the cities and on their developed agricultural estates. In our times immigrants are not quite slaves, but they are desperate to find freedom from overpopulation and poverty. In the first century there was a general break-up of the structures of government. People became disillusioned with their political leaders, and did not trust governments to provide a moral basis for society. There was strong growth in international commerce, and this created a 'common' language by which traders conversed. Currently this language is some form of English, whereas in the first century it was *Koine* Greek. There was a search for a new moral code to bring peace and decency to a corrupt society. Libertarianism was being challenged, and reason and maturity were given new priority. The dislocation of people led to a search for fellowship, community and self-respect. Such fellowships needed to be locally based and internationally recognized.

A RELIGION FOR SOCIETY

The Christian Faith was able to respond to such basic needs in society. The human spirit was restless and hungry for that which would satisfy its basic desire – to relate to God and to neighbour in fullest harmony. In such a search Christians still find themselves confronted by a multi-faith and pluralistic world. The human search for God has resulted in a number of religious responses. Among these are the monotheistic religions – Judaism, Islam and Christianity – with a belief in the oneness and holiness of God and with strong moral codes. Others include the Buddhist and Hindu religions, which aim at the rejection of the present life to win the hope of a better, freer life for the soul. Many other 'traditional' religions are closely tied to local culture and nature, and some people are returning to them as bulwarks against the pressures of international secularism. The history of the first century mirrors our current times, when many ideologies and faiths compete for an audience and committed followers. Christians today have no need to shrink back in such a climate. The Faith has always been ready to compete in the marketplace of human ideas, and to gain its adherents by the attractiveness of its truth. Christians have also been ready to listen to others and to recognize God's revelation to them. At the same time they have remained faithful to the centrality and uniqueness of God's revelation in Christ. In the year 2000 Christians can rightly claim priority in the celebrations, without keeping at a distance those of other faiths or of no faith who want to join them in giving thanks for these 2000 years of human history. Christians will also invite others to commit themselves to a future where human humility, harmony and moral integrity are key values.

SHARING GIFTS ACROSS THE GLOBE

The interdependence of humanity is being recognized more and more, helping us to draw on the strengths of others within the family of Christian peoples worldwide. Various cultures have different contributions to make in accordance with the cultural attributes which are embedded in their expression of the Faith. In the Introduction I referred to the rhythm of

Africa, the tradition of reason and reflection in Europe, the mysticism and symbolism of Eastern Christianity, the magnificence and grandeur of American expressions of worship, the sense of the Creator in the life of the peoples of the Pacific, the contemplative and compassionate under-standing of suffering in the Indian subcontinent, and the sense of the corporate among the multitudes of Asia and China. This summary gives a broad sweep of the variety to be found among Christians worldwide.

As the global village draws us closer together it is possible for Christians to bring their neighbour's worship into their mind's eye and feel its spirit to enliven their local worship. The reason for doing this in the year 2000 is not simply to enrich our worship but to witness to the international extent of Christian fellowship. Our worship and our faith will be enhanced because these strengths, which reflect particular cultural emphases, are also responses to a deep variety of needs within each individual. Often our worship speaks only to part of our personality, and ignores more hidden but equally real needs. The both/and principle should be at work again. We need to express ourselves in worship in a way which is most appropriate for our culture. *And* we can include in our worship the strengths of other cultures which meet the needs of another side of our personality. The Pentecostal vibrancy of the small congregation of South America or South Africa needs to find a balance for such worship in a focused silence, which I found so powerful while worshipping with the Taizé Community in France. Likewise the regulated formal worship so beloved in rational Europe needs to be coloured by the warmth and freedom evident in worship in the Caribbean.

A FUNERAL FOR A PRINCESS

A good example of a successful blend of styles in worship was seen world-wide in the televised funeral service for Diana, Princess of Wales. The measured steps of the pall-bearers spoke of the heaviness of the tragic death of one so full of life for others. The solo voice and plaintive music of Elton John's specially written version of 'Candle in the Wind' touched hearts and released tears of sorrow and compassion. Her brother's strong words of moral righteousness drew sustained affirmation in applause. The innocent voices of the young choir-boys carried our hopes for future generations. The resurrection trumpet continued to sound through the words of Scripture and the notes of music. This service met many deep needs in the vast number who shared in it in one way or another because it sought to be inclusive of the variety of human emotions experienced in the face of death. The service cannot be copied in full for others, for their circumstances will be different, yet it will influence Christians worldwide by posing the question: 'How can we express in worship before God all the faith and all the feelings that we, individually and corporately, need to express at such times?' This prepares us for the important task of planning worship for any occasion.

AFRICA

My travels throughout the world over the last decade have helped me reflect on such a question as I have had the privilege of sharing in worship in many different settings. Let me share some of those experiences in the remainder of this chapter.

My first experience is from Africa. This vibrant continent has a vast variety of countries and cultures, but I have always been struck with the constant array of its colours and the enthusiasm of its many peoples. There is a common effervescent spirit that bubbles forth and a deep generosity in the interchange of ideas. My first contact was with an Anglican priest from Tanzania, who came to the Church in New Zealand to stimulate our sense of mission towards our own people. We had long prided ourselves on the traffic of missionaries away from our shores. Now it was time to receive one coming in the opposite direction, to learn rather than to teach. And learn we did, of the gift of laughter and the joy of conversation, of ways of openness and boldness in bringing the Gospel message to others as a rich gift, not a poor duty. We learnt how to issue a challenge to allow a person to admit they were not a Christian without indicating that they were uncivilized. We saw in action a man who trusted in God's power of goodness and love at work across the globe. When it came to worship the same vibrancy, trust and enthusiasm were evident. Our staid ways were jolted into life, and we were encouraged to move our hands, feet and bodies to give thanks to the Creator, who gave us the breath of life.

My second experience of Africa was taking part with Archbishop Desmond Tutu in a ten-day session to plan an international conference. The members of the group had been selected from around the globe to reflect the diversity of approach to be found among the family of Anglican churches. We each brought our expertise and our cultural roots to share them with each other. I had heard a lot about Desmond, but had never met him until that conference. As soon as he walked into the room you were aware of his presence because, though small in stature, he was a giant in spirit. An infectious laugh and a deep commitment to the 'other' – both to God and to human beings – drew the attention of those around him. Later in a public gathering with this remarkable man I was not surprised when many ordinary folk wished to touch him, for by doing so they felt that they would be in touch with an example of lively holiness. The human body had become the vehicle of the Divine Spirit. The words he shared were vibrant, penetrating and hopeful. You realized in his presence that things were going to happen, and when he prayed you knew things were moving by the grace of God and the transformation of people.

My third experience of Africa was the fulfilment of a dream to worship on their soil and in their culture. The spot I chose was Soweto on the outskirts of Johannesburg. It was Holy Week and Easter, and we would pass from death to life in one of their churches. St Hilda's Church in Senaoane shared with us the worship of the crucified and risen Lord with tears of sorrow and tears of joy. Here was worship in which the whole person was engaged – body, mind and spirit. We traced the pathway to the Cross and grave; we heralded the coming of the light of life amid the darkness of death; and we sang and danced to accompany the road to resurrection. The rhythm of Creation was matched by the rhythm of the singing. Drums, clapping and a strong beat banged out on vinyl cushions gave energy to our song. On Easter Day the singing turned to dancing during the offertory procession. This was African. This was Gospel joy. This was the cultural context for the Universal Sacrament of shared bread and outpoured wine to greet the Risen Lord. Yet the worship responded to more than cultural norms. It allowed the full range of emotions to be expressed in worship. In this way it was an example from which all Christians could learn. Such worship was alive with feelings as well as with messages for the mind. It involved the use of other movements as well as of the lips. I am sure that Christ would have danced with us in joy on that Easter Day in the heat of Soweto.

ENGLAND

I flew directly from Johannesburg to London, and travelled on to Oxford. I was apprehensive that the contrast in worship styles from one Sunday to the next might confuse me. What greater contrast could I experience than between an outgoing and exuberant congregation in Senaoane and a refined, restrained and reasonable Cathedral community in Oxford? Both had a strong Christian faith. Both had choirs to lead the singing. Both cele-brated the same sacrament. Each portrayed their cultural heritage, and each needed the balancing principles of the other to meet the total needs of those at worship. Extroverted exuberance needed restraint so that it did not become disorderly. Restraint needed vibrancy so that it did not become the empty shell of formalism.

At Oxford the refinement of worship and architecture spoke of the continuity of the Faith over many centuries, and the transcendence of the Holy One, soaring like the music and the arches above us. Here there was no way that we could reduce the worship of the Divine to 'mateyness' and modernity. Our minds were drawn beyond the present to link with the past and the future. Heaven became a possibility in such perfection for ear and eye. What we heard was reasonable to the mind and helped to satisfy the search for what was consistent with the best outcomes of human thought. The Word was proclaimed with a view to the truth and to its prac-tical implementation. In this English cathedral my emotions were given space by encouraging them to grow, rather than by forcing them in violent activity. The energy was to be expressed in my soul rather than in my body. The prayers were deep and pointed as I was asked to face the issues of a broken world with passionate involvement of mind and heart – and even a hand in my purse. The choir and organ music allowed time for reflection on Divine truth, and the congregational singing gave opportunity for each voice to offer adoration and petition. This congregation was a mixture of regular members and visitors drawn from many parts of the country and beyond. Clear instructions in print, and an order of service which was easy to follow, bound us together in participation. Where the words for the music were in Latin, a translation was always provided alongside. I felt that I shared in this service with ease and dignity, and from just the right respectful distance for the worship of the Almighty God of eternity. The College and Cathedral tradition provided, with excellence, for many of my needs at worship.

In England I also had the opportunity to share in worship in a lively suburban parish, among intelligent and enthusiastic people drawn to this style of worship from a large surrounding area – sometimes crossing over other parishes to reach this one. Here was a group of like-minded people who had gathered into one worshipping congregation because it met their particular needs for strong, firm faith, joyful praise and earnest petition in prayer. For these people there was no doubt that God was present and active in their midst. The Bible revealed this God, and its words were as true now as when they were written. Here people knew each other so that at the Peace there was instant and intimate recognition of the Christ in one another. This congregation was warm to its visitors as a close-knit family would be to its guests. Yet guests they would remain until they committed themselves personally and fully to the Head of the family – Jesus Christ, Saviour and Lord. If this happened there would be fervent rejoicing that another shared in the Kingdom. Strong ethical teaching was at the heart of their worship, and the singing was a sign of affirmation, commitment and joy. A follow-up to this worship was made in the many fellowship groups that met the particular needs of enquirers, children, youth, aged, and those who wanted to share further in Bible study or prayer. The clergy/lay dividing wall had been lowered, and only the sacramental words for the Communion were reserved to the priest. However, leadership was clearly hierarchical and in this family the team-leader priest was its head.

In the balance required for good worship this experience focused on the value of the Scriptures, the goal of drawing people into faith and fellowship, participation in prayer and action, and the provision of small groups to follow up worship. All this was fired with the power of the Holy Spirit, giving warmth and enthusiasm to the words and music of the worship. In such a plain, homely setting the emphasis was on the words rather than on the space or the symbols.

WORSHIP IN THE ORTHODOX CHURCH

My experience of the worship of the great family of Orthodox churches – predominantly the Russian and Greek, is very limited, but has left me with some deep, lasting impressions. With the increasingly free movement of people between Eastern and Western Europe, and the settling of peoples from Russia and Greece in the major international cities, we are more aware of the valuable contribution to worship that these churches can make. Since the sixth century the Orthodox Patriarchs representing the regional churches of the East have all been in communion with the Patriarch of Constantinople. The Armenian Church was the first national church in Christendom and began in Cappadocia in the late third century. The history of these churches is fascinating, but it is the common threads in their worship which concern us in this book.

The use of icons has spread widely from its beginning in Orthodox worship. Icons are symbolic pictures which allow us to enter the mystery of faith through representative figures. These, painted in a stiff, formal Byzantine manner, become a window for the soul to gaze on the face of the members of the Holy Trinity, or the Blessed Virgin Mary, or another member of the venerated Saints. The pictures are painted according to a strict code in a flat dimension. For the sake of protection, especially in the Russian tradition, parts of the picture are covered in metal, leaving only the face and hands free as the focus of devotion. The popularity of icons in Western countries has grown as their purpose as an aid to meditation has become more fully understood. They are not objects of divinity but channels of Divine presence and grace. The icon is venerated for the way it can put us in touch with the holiness of God and the Saints. It permits the soul to have something tangible to use as an expression of faith in the Divine. The value of icons is that the representation is created in a style which cannot be confused with realism. God the Holy Trinity is not *like* the famous icon *The Trinity* (by the fourteenth-century Russian artist Andrei Ruboev), but this icon has helped many to enter into the mystery of the unity of the Godhead while at the same time acknowledging the reality of God as Father, Son and Holy Spirit. Mathematical formulae and scientific fact will not help anyone discover the power and the meaning of the Trinity, but an icon can assist us to 'know' this mystery and relate to the totality of God. The Community at Taizé in France has incorporated the use of a variety of icons into its large worship space. These have provided intimate points of reflection for the pilgrims seeking to enter more deeply into the experience of God through personal and corporate worship. I also experienced the value of icons when staying at a Greek Orthodox hostel at Geneva while attending a meeting at the World Council of Churches. Here the icon depicted a saint, and this was a major factor in helping me to understand the place of the community of saints in our daily worship. Saints were not consigned to history, but were part of the present worship of God by the one Church in heaven and on earth. The presence of this icon witnessed to that reality. My struggle for holiness and maturity was caught up in the hope of perfection in the holy ones of every age.

In AD 988 the Russian Emperor Vladimir established Christianity as the official religion of his empire. One thousand years later, at the time of the Lambeth Conference of Bishops in 1988, the Archbishop of Canterbury invited the Patriarch as part of the anniversary celebrations to hold a service in Canterbury Cathedral. My enduring memories of this service were of the veneration of an icon with the use of plenty of incense, and of the magnificent singing of the Litany by the London Orthodox Choir and their cantor. Here the sense of continuity and mystery in prayer and worship was very evident. There was a timeless quality in this worship which spoke of the graciousness of God down the centuries, and of our trust in God for the future of the Church and the human race. There was nothing small or limiting about this worship. The voices echoed and re-echoed around the walls so that peal upon peal of prayer sounded forth in hopeful petition. The symbol of incense carried these prayers to the throne of heaven, and, caught up in the prayers of Christ, we found grace to help in our time of need.

Features from the service of Baptism in the Orthodox tradition are influencing the practices of other churches. A variety of symbols highlight the meaning of this sacrament. Oil, candle-light and water are all used to tell of the healing, guidance and fullness of life which God offers through the power of these symbols. Too often in the past in other churches restraint in the ways these symbols are used has reduced them to mere tokens. The quantity of the substance has been reduced to the minimum and the actions have been passed over at speed. Words have been multiplied as holy symbols have been marginalized. We should note that the oil is for anointing the body, not to leave a thumb print; that the candles are to be lifted as a light on a hill, not burning dimly in a corner; that the water is ample and deep like a flowing river or a gushing spring, so that the baptized becomes wet enough to have to be dried. There can be no sprinkling of water, with a drop dripping from the fingers as if the water would hurt the recipient. In Orthodox worship these symbols speak at the level of the heart as well as the mind. Sight, touch and smell evoke the full range of our senses. These symbols, fully used, allow the worship to be experienced as a 'grand occasion' signifying the overwhelming actions and graciousness of God. In the Orthodox practice the unity of the sacraments of Baptism and Eucharist is made clear. Membership of the church opens the door to the Eucharistic Feast, whatever the age of the person baptized. The family of the baptized is not limited to the human relations, but to the whole Church, of which this gathered congregation is the local representative. The venerated icons remind everyone that the Saints of every age also form part of this universal Church into whose fellowship this person is baptized. We perceive this not because we are so informed, but because the symbols tell our senses this is so. The sights and sounds impress themselves deeply upon the soul.

THE USA

There are many Orthodox congregations in the USA, but my travels there have put me in touch with another set of experiences which I believe can add a further dimension to our understanding of worship. From that vast continent I have chosen to reflect on two places which I have visited. One is the Washington National Cathedral and the other is a small parish church in Los Angeles.

The National Cathedral in Washington stands high on a hill overlooking the state buildings and memorials on the slopes far below where the land falls away to the Potomac River. As no skyscrapers are allowed in this capital city, the twin towers of this Gothic-design building witness to the elevation of God over the works of mankind. Inside the great nave has a clear span leading the eye to the sanctuary of the high altar. On each side hang banners representing all the dioceses of the nation. Gazing up at the vaulted ceiling, you can just see the outline of the embossed endings to the arches, but the height is so great that you can only wonder what the symbols might mean. Stained-glass windows circuit the nave and in brilliant colours stretch skyward. In one is set a piece of moon-rock brought back from a space mission. Above the entrance is the circle of the Rose Window, adding to the brightness of the sun's rays. In this building space and size are used to portray the magnificence and grandeur of God. Even the moon has been brought down to size so that nothing can rival the greatness of the Creator. During my visit the tourists and pilgrims seemed to stand or walk slowly around the space in a daze, overwhelmed by the magnitude of it all – and of the God who was the source of its inspiration. I was glad to have a friendly guide to show me the glories of the place and lead me into some of the side chapels, which were sanctuaries of personal prayer and reflection. There 'humanizing' art brought the God of the heavens down to a size to which I could more easily relate. The striking feature of these wall-paintings was that the Christ of Nazareth was set among the Saints of this cathedral's history. This concept was again obvious when we moved to the high altar and observed its reredos wall carved in white stone. In the centre was the figure of the Christ, ascended in majesty and seated on the throne. With one hand he blessed the nation, with the other he held the sceptre of authority surmounted by the Cross. In the rows of niches all around the Christ were the stone-carved figures of the Saints of every age and every part of the globe. There was no national limit to this interpretation of the whole Church. It crossed the continents, even to the depths of the South Pacific to remember its early missionary bishops Selwyn and Patteson, and two of its priests and martyrs, Taratoa and Taroniara.

My visit to this Cathedral gave me a renewed realization of the majesty of God and the magnitude of the Creator. It reminded me of the concept of a Christian nation faithful to its founding pilgrims, and their determination to find true religion and an opportunity to put it into practice for the welfare of themselves and all who would join them in this new nation. This Gothic building, set in a new land, made clear to me that our expressions of Christianity might be new, but our roots are deep and ageless. Just as the buildings on the Capitol Hill repeated the Corinthian columns of Greece and the dome of Rome to signify the roots of democratic civilization, so this Gothic Cathedral helped the nation's church to feel in touch with the glories of the past ages of faith. As the orb held in the Ascended Christ's hand had a Cross on top of it to signify that Christ had come to save the world, so this congregation would be called in worship to be part of the international mission to the far corners of the globe. If the moon-walk mission could be fulfilled, so the mission of the Gospel could be equally accomplished. In this Cathedral Christ would stand in prayer for and over the nation. Each part of it was present through its banner, and all would be gathered together in prayer for freedom, justice and truth to prevail through faith and hope.

For many hours we flew over this continent until we reached its Pacific coast, and there on the next Sunday we were welcomed in a small family church in one of the suburbs of Los Angeles. If national unity and pride is one pillar of the establishment in the USA, the family is the other. These are the twin communities of concern. This was clearly reflected in this parish which had resisted the temptation to express itself in large buildings, and instead had felt the need to worship in a smaller space, where all the family could feel at home. The congregation represented all the range of family ages, from babes in arms to the frail aged in wheelchairs. Both genders were equally represented among the clergy and the laity. The worship was bright and engaging, and the Word was intelligible and practicable. From the young to the old, from all races, we took our place at the one table. After the service there was a lot of sharing of news and views, both outside the church in the sunshine while the children played on the grass, and inside in a social lounge which acted as a drop-in centre during the week. The prayers of the people during the service reflected the social aspects of the Gospel as well as family matters, and these prayers were supported by practical assistance to those in need. It seemed here that the old adage 'The family that prays together, stays together' might come true.

THE VILLAGE CHURCH OF THE PACIFIC

If you cross the Pacific Ocean from this west coast of America you reach the various scattered island groups in the Pacific. To the north of New Zealand and Australia you find the Solomon Islands lying not far below the line of the Equator. Here is a nation which is predominately Christian, and whose worship is centred on the village community. Morning and evening the village church, made of leaf panels, calls the local people from their houses and their gardens to worship God with prayer and praise. The rhythm of life is reflected in the rhythm of prayer. Sunrise and sunset, day and night, are in the care of the Creator God. Worship here is closely linked with living in God's Creation. The prayers are for the safety of those fishing at sea and for a successful harvest from the gardens on the land. Thanksgiving is offered to God for the safe delivery of a child, and for the life of an old person who has died and must be laid to rest in the grave. Life is simple and hard, with few possessions to divide people from the gifts of God in Creation – air, water, food, shelter and contentment to enjoy them. In these village churches the children play quietly on the sand-covered floor until they are old enough to join the others who repeat the prayers and hymns from memory. The struggle of life is never easy, and the fabric of society can be quickly rent asunder by sin, but God is yet present to sustain and to forgive. The essence of worship is to acknowledge the source of life and the power of God to shape the day-to-day world. The exuberant joy of the village feast day, when the patron saint of the church releases everyone for celebration, contrasts with other occasions of solemnity when there must be a search for new hope. This occurs after a cyclone has swept before it everything which lies in the path of its storm – churches, houses, community buildings and gardens. The importance of worship for this community is shown by the cleanliness of the building and the newly washed clothes worn by those attending. Worship is never undertaken casually, and time and effort go into training those who participate. It is a sacred privilege to be a village priest, deacon or catechist, and even to be a reader, server, acolyte, censor or prayer leader is a high honour. Each has a role to play and that part must be done to perfection within the limits of ability. All can offer praise and sing:

> Let all the islands rise and sing,
>   and to our God their praises bring;
> On strings and drum your might proclaim,
>   sound the glory of your name;

Pa-se-fi-ka, Pa-se-fi-ka,
   with throbbing reef and coral shore,
for fish and shell and mighty whale,
   for all your gifts our thanks we pour.[2]

INDIA

Mother Teresa of Calcutta will be remembered as one of the Saints of the twentieth century for her work for the dying and the poor, first in India and then in many parts of the world. This Albanian-born nun incarnated some of the basic qualities of the people of the continent where she worked and lived for so many years. Resilience in the midst of suffering, quiet contemplation of the Divine, and a loving compassion for those who are hurt, are all the mark of the contribution of Indian Christianity to the world of faith. As Malcolm Muggeridge wrote in the early 1970s, Mother Teresa shared with all 'a spirit so indomitable, a faith so intractable and a love so abounding'.[3] These qualities should be the hallmarks of all our worship. The attraction of Mother Teresa lay in the way she and her community combined reflective prayer and responsive action. Her doing and her praying were all of one piece. She would find Christ in the world of the poor and the dying as much as in the Sacrament of the Altar. So she would pray:

> Dearest Lord, may I see you today and every day
> in the person of your sick,
> and, while nursing them, minister to you.
> Though you hide yourself behind
> the unattractive disguise of the irritable,
> the exacting, the unreasonable,
> may I still recognize you and say:
> 'Jesus, my patient, how sweet it is to serve you.'
> Lord, give me this seeing faith,
> then my work will never be monotonous.
> I will ever find the joy of humouring the fancies
> and gratifying the wishes of all poor sufferers.[4]

Her sustaining power to work such miracles of love was her silent contemplation of God.

God is the friend of silence…
The more we receive in silent prayer,
the more we can give in active life.
We need silence to be able to touch souls.
The essential thing is not what we say,
but what God says to us and through us.
All our words will be useless unless they come from within…
Words which do not give the light of Christ increase the darkness.[5]

Out of the crucible of silent prayer was cast the firmness of faith that in God nothing was wasted and nothing was lacking to face the task ahead. Much of our worship needs to be inspired by such an indomitable spirit. Too many of us give up on our struggle to worship more effectively, to pray more passionately, and to act with greater compassion. The spirit of India and the spirit of the Mother of Calcutta gives strength to persist in overcoming all obstacles. If everything cannot be done at once, then each obstacle must be tackled one at a time. Each person in need is an opportunity from God. Each opportunity is a cause for prayer and thanksgiving. Prayer will turn the tide and gather the force of goodness into a momentum which will sweep all evil before it.

ASIA

The peoples of Asia are as numerous and diverse as the peoples of the Indian subcontinent. It is important for the world community to recognize their influence and to see their contribution to a corporate understanding of life and faith. My experiences of the Christian communities of Asia are again limited, even though many people from the countries of that continent are now my neighbours in New Zealand. My contacts have come through visits to Singapore, Hong Kong and Japan, and through my work in leadership training for Anglican bishops and teachers of theology in the region. The expansion of the Christian churches in Asia in the last decade has been remarkable. Though small as a percentage of huge populations, the Christian communities are still sizable in numerical strength. Mission has been firmly rooted as a principle of church life and worship, and boldness is a mark of the proclamation of the Gospel.

However, what I want to emphasize in this chapter is the sense of corporate identity which I always experience within an Asian congregation. The many become one in the presence of God. There is a discipline and a unity which give the lie to individualism as a norm in Christian teaching. There is strong respect for each person, but only as part of the whole. My experience of congregations in Asia is that all are attentive to the purposes of the moment, and even younger children seem to understand that they must concentrate on the task of worship. No one is left out. The ushers make sure that all have a seat and an order of service. After the worship there is a strong sense of fellowship and friendship. Greetings are shared, and in Singapore I found that a refreshing drink and light food were provided for all who would stay. There was no sense here that I had had an individual time with God in the worship and would quietly withdraw after the service in case my neighbour broke my links with God by their conversation. We, not I, had worshipped and now we would naturally care for one another in conversation and compassion.

The call of mission was strong in all my experiences of worship among congregations in the various parts of Asia. They took seriously the responsibility to help others hear the Gospel which had touched their lives, and which they knew would redeem the lives of all. They had heard in worship about the Good News of Jesus Christ, which would bring fresh hope to a society where luck and money tried to fill the vacuum caused by secularism. In Christian worship each was affirmed as having a place in God's community, and each was given strength to share the Gospel with others in the community of the nation.

LEARNING FROM OUR INTERNATIONAL NEIGHBOURS

We have travelled across the globe in a speedy survey. Space does not permit me to fill out the details of these pen pictures, but I hope that they provide sufficient insights into the contributions that we can receive from one another for the betterment of our worship. We can hold hands with our sisters and brothers across the globe and find new ways and renewed strength to bring a full balance to our worship. There is much in this survey which will enable us to broaden our horizons to discover new ways to meet the needs of all our emotions in worship, and to warn us not to disregard essential aspects of mission and ministry that flow from our worship.

The Revelation of St John (7:9, 11–12) unveils a vision of the whole Church at worship:

> After this I looked, and there was a great multitude that no one could count, from every nation, from all tribes and peoples and languages,

standing before the throne and the Lamb. And all the angels stood … and fell on their faces before the throne and worshipped God, singing: 'Amen! Blessing and glory and wisdom and thanksgiving and honour and power and might be to our God for ever and ever! Amen.'

As we take up our celebrations of worship for the year 2000 we need to hold on to the breadth of this vision, and reflect the peoples of our world in all their variety in our worship. This will signal the international nature of our Christian Faith as we give thanks for its spread from its homeland in Israel/Palestine to the ends of the world. The emphasis in liturgy always lies in our worship of God, but it can also incorporate our unity in praise, prayer and petition with our fellow Christians in all parts of the world. In this way, as one family in Christ, we can hold each other's hands across the globe.

5

WORSHIP FOR A
NEW MILLENNIUM

In our local shopping centre one of the retail firms has installed a digital millennium clock on the wall outside the main entrance. It will show the local temperature, the local time, and a count-down clock showing the days, hours, minutes and seconds to the beginning of the year 2000. This is the new age of technology providing instant connections worldwide through email conversations, and global media pictures of disasters on the television screen in your own living-room. In such an environment it is natural that people are asking questions about the use of different forms of media as part of the worship in their local church.

One of the 10 questions that we raised in the Introduction was: *In a multi-media age how can we use liturgical art, dance and drama to connect the Jesus of history with the Christ of our worship?* My first response is to say that it is vital that we do include activity for the eye as well as the ear in our worship. It was a tragedy for the Church that the puritanical reformers destroyed such a wealth of art, sculpture and colour in their drive to rid the Christian Church of the abuses of transacting money for prayer and worshipping idols in place of God. However evil these were, the reformers left us with a legacy of poverty for the eye in worship when they threw out beauty with the beast, and destroyed many of the artistic symbols that so enhance worship. The previous chapter showed how important symbolism, drama and art are to the cultural expression of worship, and how they can enrich worship in another culture through sensitive borrowing.

It will be important for our celebrations in the year 2000 to create in each local setting a suitable symbol for this important year and for the special acts of worship which will mark the start of the new millennium. In my mind's eye I can imagine a large display area in the foyer of the worship space in which a picture of the Church of the Annunciation at Nazareth or the Church of the Nativity at Bethlehem is linked with a ribbon to a map of the world marking the location of such churches in the lands of Palestine/Israel. Another picture, this time of our own local church, will be linked by a different coloured ribbon to our place on the globe. Above the map there will be a picture by one of the great artists of previous centuries showing Jesus Christ with the Apostles and Saints. To the left of this picture will be a collage of photographs of the holy ones of this generation, and to the right some photographs of the local congregation at work in worship, learning and mission. On a table under the display board there will be a set of Bibles, one in each of the local languages, and they will be opened at the birth narratives in Luke or Matthew. Also on the table will be a framed prayer for the new millennium composed by the senior children of the congregation – the generation who will see the most of the new century. Also on the table is a diary of events showing the occasions of witness and service to be carried out by members of this congregation. This whole display is regularly 'kept alive' by changing the symbols of celebration with the use of cards, flowers, candles in various colours, ribbons, flags and mobiles.

As an alternative for congregations more technologically minded I can see a video unit set up in the foyer with a special set of video displays programmed at the touch of a button. The first video is from the Holy Land showing the significant places for Christian pilgrimage – Nazareth, Bethlehem, the River Jordan, Capernaum, the Sea of Galilee, the Church of the Beatitudes, the Jesus Boat, and the places of Christ's passion, death, resurrection and ascension in and around Jerusalem. The second video is of the activities of the local congregation – its worship, its educational programme, its outreach and evangelistic opportunities, its service and pastoral care, its preparation for participation in the sacraments of Baptism and Eucharist, its small groups for spiritual development, and a set of profiles of its clergy and key laity. The third video is of the activities of its link congregation in another part of the world, showing insights into their particular ways of expressing their culture in worship, mission and ministry.

During the year 2000 such a congregation would no doubt film and edit a video showing the main acts of celebration, and capturing on film a variety of messages of hope for the initial years of the new millennium from members of the congregation and community, culminating in some plan for future action to enhance the community and the local church's worship and mission in the next decade.

In some sense all liturgy is dramatic. It plays out with words and actions the story of the initiatives of God towards humanity, and the responses we make to God's grace. It is obviously possible to read the Scriptures as drama, where the scene is set and the players come and go, portraying the truth in word and symbolic action. We have come to realize that stories can be a good way of telling the truth, and sometimes better than 'factual accounts' where the facts themselves tell us nothing but the facts. Much of our worship will be enlivened by adding some touch of drama to the occasion.

A wedding service is a good example of how the dramatic and symbolic add power and sanctity to the spoken words. In a secular version of a wedding, two people can sign a document and make a simple vow in front of witnesses and a legal official. It is all over in minutes and the social contract is fully binding. A wedding service, however, provides the means of enhancing each part of the action and of acknowledging that God's love inspires our human love to blossom in rich complexity as it unites two persons into mature oneness.

What is true of a wedding is equally true for other occasions of worship. Drama allows us to have time to see the significance of the words and actions, and opens a window for God's grace to shine through onto our human endeavours. Liturgical dance can highlight certain aspects of liturgy such as the Gospel reading, the offertory procession, the Lord's Prayer, and the dismissal. Such drama and dance is never a 'show' but an extension of the offerings of worship on behalf of the whole congregation. The dancers or the players are not performing for an audience, but are representatives in expressing the feelings and responses of all those engaged in worship. As the dance is very closely connected to culture, it is an important way of incarnating the Christ as part of a particular group within the whole of humanity.

PLANNING FOR 'WORSHIP 2000'

Now it is time to address another question raised in the Introduction: *How can we avoid each Christian denomination or church competing with its neighbour, and instead plan for a unified Christian celebration of the new millennium?*

Diversity has always been a mark of the Christian community from the very beginning of the expansion of the Church. Christians from the Jewish and Greek cultures were soon joined by those from Rome, North Africa, Persia and Asia Minor. Later, in Great Britain, there was a clash between the Celtic and Roman strands of Christianity, which had some major differences in worship practice and church government. Uniformity has sometimes been attempted within one national church structure – usually when church and state closely overlap. In our present age diversity of custom and culture is widely accepted within the Christian community, though it is sometimes a problem-causing division at a local level.

Yet there are times when Christians need to gather as *one* family in order to witness to the essential unity of faith that binds them together. I believe that one of those times is now upon us with worship to mark the start of the new millennium. In this way Christians can show the community just how much diversity there is among Christians, and yet at the same time how they can unite for key events. In some of the earlier chapters I have indicated that it would be best if at each level of the community – from nation to tiny local groups of neighbours – there were an opportunity for a combined celebration *and* also an opportunity for the individual Christian congregations in their own churches to note in worship this unique year in the life of humanity. Such concepts require forward planning, goodwill and cooperation, and strong leadership for coordination. It will be a real blessing to our Christian communities if such planning and cooperation takes place, for it will assist ongoing mutual understanding and a sense of common purpose in witnessing to the non-believing world. I am sure that the results will be seen in some joint ongoing projects to show God's love and concern within the wider community. 'Cooperation not competition' has become a catch-cry for politicians as well as for those who proclaim the Gospel. Cooperation should be a key attitude in all the activities for the year 2000, and in this Christians can give a lead. Already I hear that networks for cooperation are in place at many levels, from the World Council of Churches and its affiliate churches to the national conferences of churches and even local ecumenical bodies. These are starting-points only, as not all Christian ecclesial communities belong to such groupings. It is important that all Christians are invited to participate, and *to be part of* the cooperative planning. When this book goes to print in early 1999, it is hoped that detailed planning will have already begun in most areas. It is vital that those who are already at work should check that they have cast the net widely to include all Christian groups in their invitations. Where nothing seems to be happening it is the responsibility of us all to check on the situation and take a lead if this is still necessary. During the course of the research for this book I received a great deal of information about the preparations under way. This information was often in published form from organizations covering a global span. These included Dr Konrad Raiser's book *To be the Church – Challenges and Hopes for a new Millennium* (World Council of Churches); and the Pope's Encyclical letter *On the Coming of the Third Millennium* (Vatican Apostolic Letter, 10 November 1994). These show that major planning has taken place at the international level, but this must be translated into action at the level of the local congregation.

All this planning will culminate in significant celebrations of worship and in dedicated service to God's world. Part 2 of this book contains material which has been gathered and written to provide outlines for such worship occasions, and words for praying and reading to mark the start of the new millennium.

CONTINUITY OF FAITH

Worship, as we have seen, links the past to the present, the local to the universal, and the individual to the corporate community. Worship gives us the opportunity to maintain the links which, because of familiarity, we too often pass over without proper recognition. Many of these links also hold Christians together across the globe. To restate the links here may reveal them as obvious, but it is important to do so before I outline some new directions in worship which I can see us taking in the new millennium. Our long-established links with past generations of Christians and with Christians now in other places in the world are these:

- The records of the life, death, resurrection, and ascension of Jesus Christ as told to us in the New Testament.
- Our faith that the words of Holy Scripture reveal to us the mind and heart of God.
- Our response to the outpouring of God's love which we make in the sacrament of Baptism or in an act of commitment to Jesus as Lord.
- Our unity with Christ and the Christian family through the sacrament of Communion.
- Our incorporation in the prayer of Christ, especially as we use the Lord's Prayer.
- Our acts of witness and service to humanity in the power of the Holy Spirit.

- Our readiness to share in an act of reconciliation through the generosity of God's forgiveness.
- Our affirmation in the historic Creeds of who God is and what God has done for our salvation.
- Our trust in the Holy Spirit to inspire our worship and our prayers, and to make known to us on each occasion the presence and power of God.

These fundamentals will always find a place in a full act of worship, but the language and mode of their expression will change with the passing years. Alongside these enduring foundations, each century will see new directions in worship, and as the millennium begins some new factors are emerging.

NEW DIRECTIONS IN WORSHIP

The first new direction is a return to an emphasis which was there in earlier times, but in some places has been overlooked in recent years: *Liturgy involves the use of the whole person and all of the five senses – smell, sight, hearing, taste and touch.*

This new direction is influenced by both the psychologist and the playwright. The psychologist has helped us to see that it is only as we engage all the senses that we fully participate in an activity, and in doing so evoke and collect items for the memory. The playwright creates a drama that draws us into the action and evokes the full range of the senses.

The warm smell of a place can link us to the past by memories of its association, and can invite us into the present with the aromas which declare a welcome. In agricultural communities a festival of thanksgiving at harvesttime is connected to all the similar occasions of the past by the smell of the grains, the fruits, the vegetables and the flowers. The smell of incense or the beeswax candles can often declare a space 'holy', hallowed by the prayers of continuing generations. For some people the scent of flowers in a church recalls a wedding or a funeral or a summer church festival.

The other initial sense we use as an evocative approach to worship is sight. The shape, order, style and beauty of a space for worship is taken in by the eye and transmitted to the brain to send messages of prayerful peace, of God's presence and the picture of heaven. 'O worship the Lord in the beauty of holiness' is the first line of a traditional Epiphany hymn, and it correctly brings together three key concepts – worship, beauty and holiness. An ugly building and a chaotic space destroy the spirit of holiness. If the eye cannot relate to the size and the shape of the space, the inner sense of congruity is troubled and the soul cannot be at peace for worship. The decision of the second Vatican Council to ask for attention to the arrangements of the interior space of their churches and for the removal of extraneous statues and symbols in order that there could be focus on the central actions within the Eucharist has born fruit in enhanced worship. The ecumenical community at Taizé has gone to infinite trouble to create a worship building whose interior allows the eye to focus on a space which both colours and rests the spirit, drawing the worshipper into attitudes of reflection and engagement alternately. A number of other buildings across the world have been constructed on such a large scale that they overawe the worshipper and prevent the creation of a sense of community when the numbers of those attending are not large enough to fill the whole area. In these circumstances the eye needs defined spaces to which to relate as well as taking in the sweep of the total building.

Hearing has become the most dominant of the senses used by the worshipper in modern times, but difficulties in hearing still deafen a congregation. As church buildings grew larger, so the direct link between the speaker and the listener became strained. One of the advantages of the age of communication has been the availability of technology to project the voice and sound more accurately towards the hearer. In worship such technology needs to be used with sensitivity, as it can reduce the direct relationship between speaker and congregation which is required for good worship. The personal element contained in intonation and gesture must not be lost in amplification. The equipment also needs fine adjustments to be made according to the size of the space, the numbers present and the pitch of the particular voice. Any faults create a major disturbance to the flow of worship. If it is at all possible, sight and sound should coincide, and when this is not possible the video screen has proved valuable. Music plays a significant part in worship, and the balance between voice and instrument is a key issue. A dominating organ or other instrument can drain the energy of the congregation as they attempt to be heard over the music. A supporting musical line lifts the voices so that they gain spiritual energy from their notes and words of worship.

The Christian Faith has always considered it essential to carry out the command of Jesus Christ to 'do this in remembrance of me'. The sacrament of Holy Communion is a well-loved entry into the presence of God, and is our means of sharing in the sacrifice of Christ. The recalling of the Christ is not simply by word and symbol, but also by taste. The words of a traditional Communion anthem emphasize this aspect of the Eucharist:

'O taste and see how gracious the Lord is.' The use of such language is not metaphorical but is connected with the real satisfaction to our sense of taste that comes from sharing the Bread and Wine. Attempts have been made over the years to reduce the use of the sense of taste in this sacrament for the sake of convenience or hygiene. This is a mistake on both accounts. God created us with a sense of taste and by it came the gift of discernment and of celebration. It still needs to be used in the worship of the Creator, and care should be taken to see that the Bread we share and the Wine we sip is of such quality that its taste gives a positive experience to the worshipper.

Many members of congregations at worship have discovered the importance of touch as part of the liturgy. The custom of passing the Peace has grown in many cultures because of its essential element of having 'touched' the body of another person and thereby having affirmed the interchange of love and peace. The satisfaction of this element in worship has evoked the desire for the laying on of hands to be used in intercessory prayers, especially to receive blessing, guidance, protection and healing. The act of touch in the Ordination of the clergy has always been central to the liturgical rite. It has now been extended to the commissioning of lay people to various offices, and to the 'sending forth' of church members for mission. Touch also plays a major part in the actions of anointing with oil, both in Baptism and in the Liturgy of Healing. The 'feel' of the oil is an important aspect of these practices, just as the 'feel' of the water is in the service of Baptism. Our bodies directly experience a Divine power, and faith creates the connection through the relationship between the worshipper and God. Again, in the Funeral Service touch has a role in the farewell to the dead person which we witness when many of the mourners want to touch the casket as they take their leave of it for the last time.

In any celebration of worship for the new millennium it is vital that those who are doing the planning should provide means for the congregation to use all their senses at some time or other in the occasion. The outline services in Chapter 7 give examples of how this might be achieved. The principles which I have set forth are important but the means of applying them will vary according to culture and circumstances.

The second new direction again builds on past traditions. It is this: *A variety of symbols are being used as aids to our worship*. We know that the overcrowding of symbols can be confusing to the senses, but an ordered, focused use of them is a powerful stimulant to worship. Traditionally the most common symbol in use in churches has been the Cross, in a whole variety of shapes and forms. It has long been the 'trademark' of the

Christian Faith. However, for this symbol to be kept alive there is a need for variation and supporting features. The bare wooden Cross can be draped with cloth for the Passion season, supported by a circlet of flowers for the Resurrection, illuminated by spotlights in a darkened space at a time of commitment, crowned for the Ascension, and linked to the crib with ribbons for the Nativity. Simply left on a wall, it dies through familiarity or is ignored through complacency. Likewise, it is sad that the weight of the altar table has in many Christian traditions caused this piece of furniture to be anchored to the one spot. In earlier days it was moved into prominence to highlight its symbolism as the focus of the gathering of the family of Christ when they came to feast with the Risen and Ascended Lord. This movement allowed a heightened sense of relationship to Christ and to each other in the eucharistic community. When the focus was on another symbol – such as the Bible or the Font – then the table was moved away. Similarly, the symbol of the paschal candle or the Advent wreath is more effective for being a changing symbol, noting the season of the Church's year. On the other hand, the symbol of the Bread and Wine is powerful because it is both constant and changing. Its continuity links us with the past. Its freshness makes it a renewed presence of Christ for this feast and this occasion.

To these traditional symbols we need to add signs of contemporary life and witness. Some congregations now make a basket of food part of their Offertory procession in a Eucharist so that it becomes a sign of their care for the poor and hungry in their community. Intercessory prayer can often be enhanced with suitable symbols of need and pain. These can be displayed as objects, or portrayed on posters, or projected onto a screen in slide or video form. Our prayers of meditation are often aided by the use of an icon, incense, a picture or a burning candle. Decorative banners can add colour and change to a worship space, and as in the Cathedral in Washington, they can remind the worshippers of their responsibilities. The symbols of children's learning can be incorporated into the worship space for the whole congregation to make real the children's participation. In a larger worship building symbols of local commerce and industry can create intimate spaces for recognition of the whole of life and the prayer that supports it. I remember seeing a Cross of Car Crashes – made out of twisted metal – in one of the corridors in Coventry Cathedral in the industrial heart of England. This powerful symbol gave a new meaning to the Passion and a sharpness to my prayers for those who suffer in road accidents.

In worship for the year 2000 such use of symbols will provide a powerful focus in the worship space, pointing to our celebration and our thanksgiving for the past, helping us face the possibilities and pain of the present times, and moving us with boldness and perseverance into the future.

The third new direction being taken in worship at the start of the new millennium is: *The inclusion of a blend of styles in music and movement in the same service*. Real attempts are being made to bring together music from across the generations and across the globe. Taizé chants and charismatic songs can be heard from Moscow to Melbourne; in Calcutta, Cape Town and Coventry; in Honiara, Honolulu and Hong Kong. The tape recorder and the easy flow of travel has allowed styles of worship to spread quickly and 'catch on' in places far from their origins. However, care must be taken to avoid too much influence from the internationalization of worship in case it should supplant local culture and tradition, and worship become an imported commodity without any local roots. When this happens the Christian Faith becomes a strange copy of that in a far-away place and unrelated to the current situation and local issues. For this reason I have avoided in this book providing more than an outline for the large occasions of worship for the celebration of the year 2000. All planning must be done in detail by those who will share in such worship. Where material is provided it is an example to be translated as necessary into local form and languages. Yet the sharing of ideas does show that there is a place for the mutual interchange of gifts given by God to individuals, wherever they should live across the globe. Such gifts will need to be embedded in the local and the contemporary, whether such gifts come from the past or from a distance. I have included some examples of new words and old tunes, of new words and new tunes, and of different styles in Chapter 11, 'Hymns and Songs for a New Millennium'. I have done this for two reasons. First, they are worthy gifts from their authors and composers for this important occasion and will be available for use in the many places where this music fits into the local culture. Secondly, their inclusion will demonstrate to those of other cultures the sort of themes that are suitable for 'Worship 2000'. God has given the gifts of song and music to every race, and the beginning of the new millennium gives Christians the opportunity to seek out such gifts, recognize them, and use them for worship.

Much of our music will be enhanced by rhythm and movement. I have already referred to the place of dance in worship and highlighted my delight at the contribution that rhythm made to the worship at Soweto. Here I want to stress the possibilities that arise from using three different instruments which can bring rhythm and movement into our music. These are the violin, the flute or pipe, and the guitar. In other cultures there will be local equivalents for these three instruments. These can be used so that a song is supported by the notes with a strong rhythm that lifts the emotions and evokes the realization of the presence of God. The playing of these three instruments demands more visible movement of the body than is required for the more static keyboard instruments. This encourages a sense of movement in the eye and body of the worshipper. This will often be picked up by the clap of hands or the beat of the feet to affirm the rhythm. Overdone, this becomes a distraction from the words of worship, but with the right balance it can be most effective where culture allows. I am aware that what is suitable in one place can be offensive in another, but without any movement a service of worship begins to lack 'life'.

Some movement can be achieved in every worship occasion, whether separate or attached to music. A change of body position is a real aid to prayer, whether it be to kneel or to stand. The change marks a particular activity and focuses the mind on the new task in hand. The movement of many people in a procession provides for positive involvement in the action, and can symbolize a sense of progression, change of direction, commitment and transposition into the future. It therefore lends itself as a powerful ingredient in any service planned to mark the new millennium. A procession is commonly used for the 'Stations of the Cross' service in Holy Week, and this could be the parallel for a 'Journey with God down the Centuries' as part of 'Worship 2000'. Another procession suitable for this celebration year is one of witness and prayer through the centres of commerce and civic administration which form the heart of many of our towns and cities. Prayer for the community becomes very effective by virtue of the realism of being in the place where the action occurs.

The fourth and final new direction in worship that I have noted is: *The use of the new means of communication as aids to worship.* With the explosion of the means of communication through new technology there is no good reason why churches should restrict the use of visuals to static displays or the over-head projection of texts for worship. Once the equipment is in place it can be used to introduce colour, cartoon, symbolic pictures and photographic pictures onto a suitably placed screen as an aid to worship. This will enhance visual participation. As far as sound is concerned, in many worship centres, large and small, the technology has been purchased which will allow the use of recorded music of magnificent quality. This should not replace the local musicians, but is a useful addition and can add variety. One example that comes to mind is the way small groups that meet for reflective prayer have been able to use recorded Gregorian chants as well as deep silence to focus their prayer and its relationship with the Divine.

In the last few years many churches have connected themselves to email and fax, providing rapid communication across the globe. This should facilitate links between congregations in different parts of the world, though allowance has to be made for time differences. It is now possible for a congregation in Los Angeles to email or fax a message to an island community in the Pacific, telling them that prayers have been included in the Intercessions at the Eucharist to support them as they recover from a cyclone. The reverse, of course, would happen if some major disaster such as an earthquake struck the west coast of the USA. I believe such concrete communication will make our prayers for one another much more effective as God's Spirit is released and people are given new heart to face the situation. Prayer requests are even now exchanged within a congregation, and with the use of modern technology this can be extended to link communities worldwide. It is a sign and an act of our interdependence on God and one another, and a spur to a sense of common purpose and will. Modern means of communication will also be used to establish Christian networks to combat the erosion of moral values and to plan for the care of people and the environment. Too often Christians have taken their information from the public media and failed to check the situation directly with their partners in Christ most closely involved in the 'news'. A Christian network would counteract any manipulation of the facts and distortion of the events, and would create a real sense of common understanding and purpose among Christians in every land.

Communication can take place very powerfully through the medium of art. It is to be hoped that the year 2000 will be another opportunity for the artist to provide lasting masterpieces of religious painting and sculpture which portray aspects of our Faith. The painting and sculpture of previous generations have had a profound affect on worship and religious awakening. Many of these works of art are now in public and private galleries, and it would be wonderful to see national and local communities arrange for their exhibition, along with new works, to celebrate the year 2000. Such displays could be the launching-pad for outreach and mission if local congregations would be prepared to attend as guides, pointing out the themes and the significance of the works of art to the visitors to such exhibitions.

Floral decoration and display is an art form which has drawn many people into churches and provided opportunities for presentation of the Gospel. I am sure that there will be 'fields of flowers' to mark the way into the new millennium. Such flowers need to tell the story of the

Gospel as well as witness to the beauty of the Creation and give honour to the Creator.

These four new directions are already signs for the future at the dawn of the new millennium, and I hope that their inspiration will help our acts of worship to move on to draw many more people into the worship of the God who is constantly 'making all things new'.

BASIC PRINCIPLES FOR WORSHIP

It is time to move from new directions to note some basic principles which apply to worship, wherever and however it is provided. I intend the material in this chapter to be a cavalcade of ideas which might stimulate those who are planning and participating in worship events to mark the new millennium. When putting such ideas into practice I encourage people to have the following basic principles in mind:

- The primary function of worship is to honour God in praise and adoration.
- As an outcome of this there will be the formation of a community of worshippers, which will recognize itself as God's family, linking the genders, races and generations, and being open to the guests who share the occasion but not always with full Christian commitment.
- Every person who shares in worship is a full participant and is of equal importance, even though the functions they carry out within the worshipping community will differ.
- The worship will have a sense of balance and perspective between the poles of the Divine and the human, the here and the everywhere, the now and the always, and the needs of the individual and the needs of the whole church.
- In the worship there will be an opportunity to express all our emotions and passions, with laughter and tears, rest and energy, and suffering and triumph.
- There will be space in the worship to communicate in sound and sight the message of the Gospel in Scripture and Sacrament, in applied teaching and examples of Christian action.
- The pace of the worship will allow time for the expression of energy and the stillness of silence, for re-creation and the work of intercession, which will move the worshippers towards peaks of heightened awareness of the presence and power of God in their lives.

- The outcome of the worship is directed towards mission and ministry in the lives of the worshippers.
- The times for prayer in the worship allow for the full range of prayers – confession, supplication, thanksgiving, intercession – and keep continuity with the Saints of every age, praying with us as we use the Lord's Prayer.
- The images of God portrayed in the worship are consistent with Christian Trinitarian theology, and a balance is kept between the concepts of the God 'beyond' and the God 'within', and the infinite and intimate nature of God.
- The language of the worship is gender inclusive or gender neutral in reference both to God and to humanity. Particular care is taken with pronouns in the third person singular.
- The worship is set within the vision of the Universal Church of all Christian people, and the saints of every age, country and race.

PLANNING FOR EVENTS

With these principles in mind, I encourage planning groups to meet at every level to map out the special worship events that they see as suitable to celebrate the year 2000. Such groups need to gather information from and make contact with groups beyond their particular level. For example, a city-wide group will discover what is happening at a national level and also what is planned for individual local churches within their city. This should avoid clashes of dates and the holding of events too close together. I am suggesting that Christians should take the lead in the organization and planning of the worship events on a combined Christian basis. At a national level, where some secular bodies are already at work in some places, publicity for key events for the new millennium should include the worship events and such activities as a Consultation to construct a vision and implement a plan for the first decade. The city-wide and regional celebrations should aim to be large public gatherings to proclaim the importance of Jesus Christ and the Christian Faith for the whole community. They will mark the major contributions from Christianity towards peace, education, health, research, the United Nations, and community care and welfare. Although Christians will be in the forefront of the planning of these events, they should make certain that they invite community leaders and public officials to join them in their representative capacity.

I have outlined services for two major Christian Festivals – Epiphany and Ascension – as most suitable for 'Worship 2000'. It has been suggested to me by Professor Stookey of Washington DC, USA, that a third occasion could also be suitable. He points out that the last day of the year 2000, which some see as the conclusion of the second millennium, could be the time for a community-wide and inter-faith celebration to acknowledge the past millennium and to prepare for the start of a new decade, century and millennium all in one. I can see the value of this type of event at the end of the year, which would give time for the Christian community to hold their own worship events, concentrating on the remembrance of the Incarnation and giving thanks for the spread of the Gospel globally. This would be a similar pattern to that at Christmas and New Year, when Christians celebrate the uniqueness of Christ at the Festival of the Nativity, and then join with the wider community in looking forward to the New Year with its hopes and dreams, and its opportunities of achieving the new goals that have been set, such as New Year resolutions.

During the planning for the major public events at all levels, groups will want to liaise with the media for publicity, and make certain that television, radio and newsprint (depending on what is available locally) give full coverage to the events themselves. The media have been building up interest in the year 2000 for some time, and it is right that the Christian community should offer them the opportunity to focus on the significance of the date as far as Christians are concerned, and therefore of the events that Christians hold. To make the events worthy of such widespread communication, the planning groups will have to 'think big and pray hard'. They will need to recruit people with the skills to take part in such 'public' acts of worship, and not try to satisfy individual egos. Many long hours of practice will be needed for each person and group involved in the worship so that it can be projected on a sufficiently large scale as to be effective for such a public event. The size of such events should be large enough to allow many participants to show the range of ages and cultures within the Christian community in that nation or region. There should also be the suitable equipment to link this event with its roots in history and its partners in other parts of the world, thus showing the range and depth of Christian witness.

Balancing this major ecumenical and community celebration of worship, there will be events within each congregation. Local Christians in the year 2000 will want help to become effective witnesses to the coming of Jesus Christ, and to the faith and activities of the local Christian community. I am hopeful that this book and others like it will equip

Christians for their role in this task. Christians within their own congregations will want to tell again with thanksgiving the history of their Faith –
how it began at Nazareth and spread to the point at which it touched their
lives. They will want to note how past generations have tackled the crises
that faced them – be it poverty, war, slavery, tyranny or dispossession. They
will want to link up with Christians in other areas for common support
and mutual prayer. They will need training in prayer to be faithful to the
call of God and to the will of God. They will want a real share in the activity
of the church, and to be supported by their church in their outreach and
service to the community. Part 2 of this book aims to provide some
resources for Christians individually and corporately to fulfil these desires.
The excellent messages from world Christian leaders should offer them
encouragement, and the prayers should inspire their intercessions. The
biblical readings should let God's Word speak again to our situations and
direct our actions.

The generation most excited by the beginning of the millennium will be
the young, who will see most of its first century. Youth has always believed
in a 'new world beginning from today'. Their future beckons forwards,
whereas the older members of society have lived long enough to say
'There is nothing new under the sun.' The Christian Faith is attractive to
the young, who focus on the youthfulness and enthusiasm of Jesus of
Nazareth and the sense of idealism which he proclaimed. His promise of
the Spirit to enable us to achieve what seem impossible goals attracts a
generation wanting a new self and a new society, but feeling powerless to
create them without the Spirit. I trust that the planners for 'Worship 2000'
will incorporate the skills and enthusiasm of the younger generation. I am
also convinced that the young will want to hold their own celebrations in
addition to those for the whole community. These will take place in their
own style in universities, secondary and primary schools, and among
church youth organizations. These will focus on the place of young people
in Christian witness and ministry, and on the key issues which the young
believe to be pressing in upon the world's agenda, including management
of Creation, insecurity in job opportunities, handling the media, distribution of wealth, suicide and euthanasia, AIDS and the loss of fathers, the
costs of education and health, freedom and social responsibility. I have
been delighted at the contribution of prayers by young people in some
selected schools in New Zealand, which will be found in Part 2. They show
a new perspective and freshness of approach to God.

The individual Christian will also want to mark this year with their own
special private prayers and worship. They will want to give thanks to God

for the past and its contribution to their present. They will want to take responsibility for working for the future in line with the will of God revealed by Jesus Christ. They will look to be renewed by the Holy Spirit for their part in the witness of the Church. They will pray for the Spirit's gifts to give them strength to be bold in mission and ministry. I encourage you as an individual Christian reader to set aside time during the year 2000 to develop your own strategy for the future as it directly affects you. You can do this by reflecting on the passages of Scripture and the messages from Christian leaders, and then applying what is relevant to your own situation. Your prayers will be directed in thanksgiving towards God and in petition for guidance and strength for daily living in this time of a new millennium. I am sure you will be assisted if you choose particular occasions during the year to do this, and mark them in your calendar at the beginning of the year. There seem to be three really suitable times during the year for such activities. The first is at the beginning of the Epiphany season, when we can focus on the Incarnation of Christ and his mission to the world. The second is in the week after Pentecost, when it is good to focus on the strength that the Spirit gives us for our prayers and our witness to others. The final one is the first week of Advent, when we can focus on the hopes and plans for the five years 2001–5, and listen to the will of God for our lives. In this way you, the reader, would be able to mark the year as a whole, and also divide up the various aspects of the celebration into manageable sections, attending to each in turn. As you go along, and certainly at the end, do share what you have discovered with at least one other Christian. This might be by word or letter or, in this age of communication, by fax or email to a far corner of the world.

GOD AND OUR FUTURE

In all of our special occasions of worship in the year 2000 questions will be raised about God's attitude to the future of the world. We have already noted that some Church leaders are concerned that there might be too much stress on the uniqueness of the year 2000. They fear it will encourage eccentrics to predict the 'end of the age'. Of course, there is no reason to believe that God will bring all things to a final conclusion at this date rather than at any other time. The witness of the New Testament is that the Early Church faced these same problems, and the Gospel record affirms that Jesus warned against prophecies of conclusion. He told us that Christians must leave the timing to God in faith, and plan for the future as always in God's hands. Our worship in the year 2000 should help us find the power of God for the situations that we face from day to day, to recognize the contributions and lessons of the past, and to see the importance of planning and working for longer-term goals. The Incarnation principle is always at work – where there is faith and commitment, then the Spirit of God will cause the presence and power of the God of love to be born within human beings. This Spirit will give us boldness in prayer, witness and mission, and will bestow the gifts of God on the faithful individual and on the community of faith. Through our worship and praise we can eagerly expect this renewal to happen in all of us. When this occurs there will be a new burst of energy in Christian mission and community cooperation, just as there was at the start of the second millennium. God will bring this future to completion in accordance with the Divine purpose, and at a time of Divine choice. Every Christian will be always alert and ready for that glorious day, but in the meantime will be constant in praising God and fulfilling the prayer, 'Your will be done on earth as in heaven.'

6

INTRODUCTION
TO PART TWO

Part 2 of this book is given over to liturgical material as resources for those who want to celebrate the year 2000 as the new millennium begins. James Catford, on behalf of HarperCollins*Religious,* suggested this format during the first stages of the planning of the book, and I accepted the challenge eagerly.

When it came to the actual writing I realized that I would need help to provide such a range of liturgical material, and so I wrote out a list of all the people I knew whom I could invite to participate in such a project. I was heartened and humbled by the wonderful response I received. Before I set out the material in Chapters 7–11, each aiming to meet different needs in worship, I want to record my thanks to those who have contributed.

SERVICES FOR PUBLIC WORSHIP

As a contributor and part of the editorial team for *A New Zealand Prayer Book / He Karakia Mihinare o Aoteaora* (published by Collins in 1989), I had long experience in the composition of services for public worship. Chapter 7 of the present book, 'Outlines of Services for Public Worship', draws on some published material, as is recorded in the notes to that chapter, but most of the material is my own composition. Attention is drawn to various music resources that are widely known, and to the new music gathered for this book and printed as Chapter 11, 'Hymns and Songs for a New Millennium'.

THEMES, READINGS AND PRAYERS FOR CONGREGATIONAL WORSHIP AND PRAYERS AND REFLECTIONS FOR PERSONAL WORSHIP

I quickly realized that I would need fresh ideas for congregational and personal worship. Youth has always inspired me with its sharp insights and poetic turn of phrase. I approached the chaplains of three secondary schools in New Zealand, and with their enthusiastic cooperation I received the fruits of their students' compositions by Easter 1998. I was thrilled with the freshness of their prayers – new styles and new thoughts – and immediately felt inspired to use many of them as the basis for the prayers to be included in Chapter 8, 'Themes, Readings and Prayers for Congregational Worship' and Chapter 9, 'Prayers and Reflections for Personal Worship'. I have recorded the name of the originator of the material where this was given to me, or the school where it was not. I therefore record my thanks to:

The Reverend Warner Wilder, Chaplain of King's College, Otahuhu, Auckland, and these student contributors: Arul Thavarajah; G. Rhodes; Andrew Fraser; Aneil Chchima; Shaun Sutton; T. Sullivan-Vaughan; Nicholas Moss; Ben Ford; I. Sullivan; W. Brown; D. Lyall; M. Rothwell; D. Henry; C. Stevenson; R. Johnston; J. Wong; G. Deverell; W. Ormiston; G. Williams; S. Weatherston; S. Abbott; G. Panther; William Eivers.

The Reverend Winifred Blyth, Chaplain of Diocesan School for Girls, Epsom, Auckland, and these student contributors: Miriam Bissett; Fiora Au; Sarah Allerby; Violet Kua; Samantha Marsh; Janis Cheng; Shana Chandra; Danielle Evans; Qiulae Wong; Helen Cocker; Petra Carey; Elizabeth Davies; Melanie Luen; Donna MacGregor; Sarah Gatward; Clare Morton; Julia Hanna; Rak Hee Hwang; Amy Wilkinson; Kate Walker; Katie MacKinlay; Claire Wheeler.

The Reverend Erice Fairbrother, Chaplain of St Hilda's Collegiate School, Cobden Street, Dunedin and these students who contributed as a combined group: Polly Highbee; Anna Kelly; Michalle Hagan; Rachael Elder; Anna Garland; Kylie Matheson.

In this section there are some prayers composed by my wife, Rosemary Atkins, who with friends has already produced two books of prayers published by Collins: *Linked in Prayer* and *Joined in Love*. I pay tribute to her abiding inspiration and her skilled contributions.

MESSAGES FOR A NEW MILLENNIUM

In Chapter 10, 'Messages for a New Millennium', I wanted to make certain that the voices of some key Church leaders and scholars could be heard at the beginning of the new millennium, and I was delighted that such a widely representative group of contributors agreed to send a message or to allow me to print a selection from a previously published source. Nearly all in the following list are known personally to me, or have been recruited on my behalf by my friends. I express to them all my sincere gratitude and admiration for the words they share with us as we celebrate this key occasion. So my thanks go to the following:

Cardinal Tom Williams of Wellington, New Zealand, for the Vatican material containing the extracts from the addresses of Pope John Paul II.

Archbishop George Carey, Archbishop of Canterbury, for his personal contribution to this book.

George Lemopoulos, Executive Secretary at the World Council of Churches on behalf of Dr Konrad Raiser, the General Secretary of the WCC.

Lady Christine Eames, World Wide President of the Mothers' Union.

Dr Han Wenzao, President of the China Christian Council, at Nanjing, China; and to Bishop Peter Kwong of Hong Kong, who made the links for me.

The Right Reverend Duncan Buchanan, Bishop of Johannesburg in the Church of the Province of Southern Africa.

The Reverend Dr Yeow Choo-Lak, Executive Director of the Association for Theological Education in South East Asia.

The Right Reverend Jabez Bryce, Bishop of Polynesia and Secretary of the South Pacific Anglican Council.

The Right Reverend Dr Penny Jamieson, Bishop of Dunedin in the Church of Aotearoa, New Zealand and Polynesia.

The Right Reverend Roger Herft, Bishop of Newcastle in the Anglican Church of Australia.

The Right Reverend Dr Michael Nazir-Ali, Bishop of Rochester in the Church of England, and former Bishop of Rawind in the United Church of Pakistan.

The Very Reverend John Arnold, Chairman of the Central Committee of the Conference of European Churches.

The Reverend Professor Justin Taylor SM, at Ecole Biblique et
Archéologique Française, in Jerusalem.
The Reverend Professor Frances Young at the University of
Birmingham, UK.
The Reverend Professor Laurence Stookey at Wesley Theological
Seminary, Washington DC, USA.
The Reverend Professor William Abraham at Perkins School of
Theology, Dallas, USA.
The Reverend Dr Philip Culbertson at the Auckland Consortium for
Theological Education within the University of Auckland, New
Zealand.
And a group of young students at King's College, Auckland, New
Zealand: Nicholas Moss, John Leightly, Lloyd Bahlmann and Shaun
Sutton.

HYMNS AND SONGS FOR A NEW MILLENNIUM

In Chapter 11, 'Hymns and Songs for a New Millennium', I wanted to
include just a few examples of new hymns and songs that could be sung at
worship during the celebrations for the new millennium. I sought out
from New Zealand and England those who were well known for writing
new words and music in a variety of styles. I was very fortunate to have the
willingness of busy people to make some of their compositions available.
Some wrote new words to tunes that seem ideal for the purpose; some
wrote new songs for a particular place in Chapter 7, 'Outlines of Services';
some allowed me to repeat suitable words and music which they had
published recently, and I had the inspiration one afternoon to write some
new words to an Irish tune, and on another night to add an alternative
tune to words that had been offered to me.

All those I now list are well known for their skills and have had words
and music published. I draw attention to their works and to others whom I
have discovered. However, I realize that music and culture are very inter-
woven, and planners of worship at the local level will be aware of music
that best suits their own situation. These are excellent examples from two
cultures, and I am sure they will inspire creative writing and composition
on the occasion of the new millennium.

I am grateful to a long-time musical friend in Auckland, Mr Stanley
Jackson, for playing the music over, offering me sound advice and
arranging my tune 'Compassion'.

The contributors to Chapter 11 are:

The Reverend Norman Brookes, President of the Methodist Conference of New Zealand.

The Right Reverend Michael Baughen, former Bishop of Chester and now living in retirement in London, who also arranged for the contributions from Bishop Timothy Dudley-Smith.

Matt Redman and Martin Smith, as introduced to me by the Reverend Jeremy Clark of Upton, Wirral, England, whose copyright is held by Kingsway's Thankyou Music.

Professor Colin Gibson of Dunedin, New Zealand.

Shirley Murray of Raumati near Wellington in New Zealand.

Jillian Bray of Plimmerton near Wellington in New Zealand.

And myself.

I offer my thanks to this musical team, and together we offer our work to the teams of worship leaders and to individuals as a resource for their celebrations of the new millennium.

7

OUTLINES OF SERVICES
FOR PUBLIC WORSHIP

In this chapter you will find outlines for service forms for ecumenical occasions of public worship at a national, or regional/city, or even more local community level. I suggest that there are three possible occasions in the year 2000 when such a liturgy seems most appropriate. The first two coincide with Christian Festivals – Epiphany, which falls on 6 January 2000, and the Ascension of Christ, which falls on 1 June in this year. The third occasion is at the end of the year – either at midnight on 31 December 2000/ 1 January 2001, which is the threshold of the year 2001 and, for some, the beginning of the next millennium; or during the day of 1 January 2001 when the focus will be on the future in the new century and the new millennium.

My suggestion to the Christian community is that they should choose to celebrate one of the first two occasions, and then invite those of other faiths to share fully in the last occasion as a 'service of the spirit'. This gives a faith perspective to our visions for the new millennium and allows many people to pray in their own way for the spiritual strength to implement the new visions that emerge for our society and our world.

These outlines give a 'framework' for worship and make suggestions of suitable readings, prayers, songs and hymns. Those planning the services will, of course, want to incorporate equivalent material arising out of local usage, language and culture, but these outlines should be helpful starting-points for them and should supply them with many fresh ideas. The aim is always to make local worship worthy of God and satisfying to people because the service meets their needs and widens their vision. In this spirit I offer these three outlines for public, ecumenical worship.

THE FEAST OF THE EPIPHANY (6 JANUARY 2000)

The setting

Those planning the creation of a worship space are encouraged to adapt it so that the community can have a sense of focus on the Incarnation of Jesus Christ and on the witness of the Gospel to all the nations of the globe. The *symbols* in the worship space should be of such a size that they make a visual impact from the furthest corners of the space, within the possible sight-lines. Where this is not possible and relay equipment is available, video screens can be used to bring the symbols and the service closer to the people. The symbols used within the space should be repeated in photographic form on any printed order of service.

The Christian *symbol of the Cross* should be used as an overall symbol for the worship space. This may already be established as in a church, but for this special occasion it may be highlighted by the use of spotlighting, by the addition of coloured drapes of cloth, or by making a massive floral Cross.

The *symbol of the Incarnation* can be a crib, or a poster picture of the Church of the Nativity at Bethlehem, or a display of the words of the birth narratives in the Scriptures in local languages projected onto a screen, or a statue of the Madonna and Child, or a drama group in costume. Ribbons or long strips of cloth can be stretched from 'on high' to reach down to the Incarnation symbol. A large candle on a stand should be placed near the chosen symbol.

The *symbols for the Epiphany* should be displayed around the edges of the worship space to represent the peoples of the globe who have heard of the revelation of Jesus as the Christ. It is suggested that these are suitable symbols:

- a set of posters depicting people from many different nations;
- a display of objects from various cultures;
- silhouette cut-outs of the shape of the various continents;
- children dressed in a variety of national costumes;
- copies of Scripture portions in many different languages.

A candle holder should be placed next to each of the displays.

The *seating* of the worship space might be arranged on a fan-like plan so that the symbol of the Incarnation has 'spokes' radiating outwards towards the symbols of the peoples of the globe.

Where national or regional/city gatherings have members from various ethnic groups, these people should sit together from the start of the service, and be associated with a symbol from an appropriate geographical area. In this case care should be taken to include symbols (possibly placed at each side of the front of the worship space) of nations which are not represented by any group within the congregation. It is vital that these symbols of the 'far away' are also noted by the assembly.

Microphones should be available for the worship leaders and the readers, but should not be placed in such a way as to obstruct the view of the Incarnation symbol.

The remembrance of the Incarnation

The worship begins with a *liturgical dance*. This is most appropriately done by children. The dancers enter from behind (or if necessary from the side of) the Incarnation symbol, and create a dance of welcome to the Christ Child. For the final part of the dance it is suggested that a trumpet (or other strong wind instrument) play the tune of a Christmas carol well known to the assembly. The dancers should retire from the central position by travelling outwards towards the symbols of the nations at the edges, and should remain by the various symbols in clusters. In a different cultural setting a cultural dance of welcome to an important visitor may be more appropriate in place of this suggested dance. Any dance should have the note of joy and welcome, and the music should be associated if possible with the Christmas event.

Following the dance, Worship Leader 1 moves to the microphone to call the assembly to worship with these words:

A little over 2000 years ago in Bethlehem in Judea, within the history of God's created order, a child was born to Mary, a maiden from Nazareth in Galilee, who was supported by her husband Joseph, a carpenter by trade. This child we recognize as Jesus, God's only Son, who is Christ and Lord for us, his disciples among all the peoples of the world. This is the root in history of our contemporary faith.

The assembly responds to the Leader's words with these shouts of affirmation, printed in bold type:

Let us rejoice that God is born as one of us –
Emmanuel.
Let us rejoice that Jesus is known to us as Christ –
the Anointed One.

Let us bow down and worship him as Lord –
our Saviour.
Let us call upon the Holy Spirit
  to empower our worship and our prayer.

Silence is kept for a significant time. Worship Leader 1 continues:

So raise your voices in praise and recall the birth of Jesus Christ, which marks the beginning of our era of Christian time.

The assembly sings one of the following carols about the Incarnation, led by massed choirs if available: 'O little town of Bethlehem'; 'Once in royal David's city'; 'O come, all ye faithful'; 'The Virgin Mary had a baby boy'; 'Long time ago in Bethlehem'; 'Born in the night, Mary's child'.

Four readers then come forward to microphones to share the following readings, as the assembly is seated:

Reader 1: St Luke's Gospel tells us how a man and a woman greet the infant Jesus in the Temple in Jerusalem, when Joseph and Mary bring the baby for the Rite of Purification. *(Read Luke 2:22–24.)*

Reader 2 (a man): *Read Luke 2:25–35.*

Reader 3 (a woman): *Read Luke 2:36–38.*

Reader 4: Listen to these words of encouragement from Professor Justin Taylor, who lives and works in Jerusalem today: 'Christianity is more than an idea or an ideal. It is rooted in the history of a people and of a land. It is identified with a particular human individual, Jesus Christ, who was conceived at Nazareth and born at Bethlehem, who lived in Galilee and walked the roads of Samaria, Transjordan and Judea, and who died and rose again in Jerusalem. Those of us who have the privilege of living, even as foreigners, in this land, or who have had the opportunity of visiting it, know that our way of understanding the faith has been profoundly changed by the experience. The Gospel story becomes concrete and vivid on the shores of the Sea of Galilee or in the crowded, narrow streets of Jerusalem. Even the troubled politics of this land throw light on the Bible. Read the Old Testament or the New, and you will find not peace and concord, but hostility and division, and that is the way, it seems, it has always been. The Prince of Peace was born at a time and in a place of conflict. That is part of the reason why His person and His message are still relevant, 2000 years later.'

When the readings are over a child moves forward and prays:

O Jesus, child of Bethlehem,
   once a child like me,
help me to grow as you did,
   strong in spirit and loving in all things,
looking to the future with eyes of hope,
   and depending on God in prayer.
Create a world in which all children have a chance to grow,
without their lives becoming crippled
   by poverty, neglect, violence, abuse or pain.
Jesus, may you and I together laugh at our joys
   and cry to express our pain,
for you hear our prayers and share our lives,
   today and always.

The children of the assembly affirm the prayer with their 'Amen'.

The assembly joins together in singing the new hymn, 'Great God, of ages back in time, Eternal with us now' (see page 178), or one of their own choice on a similar theme.

Worship Leader 2 leads a responsive form of *Thanksgiving for Christ's Coming*, in which the people's part is printed in bold type:

Behold I bring you good news of great joy;
Unto us a child is born; unto us a Son is given.
The Word became flesh, and dwelt among us,
We have seen his glory, the glory as of a father's only son,
   full of grace and truth.
This light shines in our darkness,
And the darkness cannot overcome it.
To you is born in the city of David, a Saviour,
Who is Christ the Lord.
How great is the love that the Father has shown to us;
We are called God's children, and such we are.
Put on the new nature, created after the likeness of God,
   in true righteousness and holiness;
In Christ Jesus we are all children of God through faith.

Thanksgiving, love and praise to you, Jesus Christ;
You are God revealed in human form.
You are the baby visited by the shepherds and the sages;
the boy in the Temple learning the law;
the man baptized by John in the Jordan River,
the Son of God driven into the desert to face the devil.
To you the angels ministered their strength,
In you the power of the Spirit overcame evil.
You are Christ the teacher, Christ the healer,
You called sinners to repentance,
   and released them from their sins.
You turned your face to Jerusalem,
and walked the way of the Cross.
By death you overcame death,
and gave your life to redeem us all.
In resurrection you were born again to live for ever;
You ascended into heaven to reign as Lord of all.
Thanksgiving, love and praise to you, Lord Jesus,
a light to the nations, and the Saviour of our world.

When the assembly is seated two chosen people come forward to tell of the significance of Christ's coming for the way it has brought a Christian contribution to such areas of life in society as education, care of the needy and health.

When they have completed their addresses, Reader 5 moves forward to a microphone and reads Isaiah 60:1–6, 'Arise, shine, for your light has come ...'

The assembly responds with a hymn or song celebrating the light of the Incarnation. Suitable hymns/songs include 'I am the light of the world'; 'Thy word is a lamp unto my feet'; 'Let there be light, let there be understanding'; 'Lord your almighty word, chaos and darkness heard'.

As the hymn/song is sung the dancers may bring candles to be lit from the tall candle at the Incarnation symbol, and take the candles back to the holder next to each of the Epiphany symbols. There the candles remain burning.

The revelation of Christ in our world today

Worship Leader 3 introduces speakers who relay or deliver messages from Christian people in four different continents of the world. They tell how the Christian Faith has been a light of hope shining in the various situations in their part of the world. These statements can be supported by video or voice recordings, or by direct communication links where the technology is available.

At the conclusion Reader 6 reads St Paul's message to the Christians at Rome: Romans 12:9–18, 'Let love be genuine ...'

Where there are a number of cultural groups in the assembly, the opportunity could be taken here to include songs by two (or at most three) groups in their own language. A translation or summary of the words should be projected onto a screen or printed in the Order of Service. Where possible these songs should have a maximum amount of rhythm so that the members of the assembly can be invited to match the rhythm with their actions of clapping or body movement. This is a time of celebration.

The new millennium

A national/ regional/ city representative is invited to address the assembly, giving a vision for their society for the new millennium. This could be introduced by use of a video (or slides) showing tokens of how society is today.

The assembly affirms the vision with a *Hymn or Song* for the new millennium. (Some examples will be found on pages 175–199.)

Six young people then come forward to the microphones. A secondary school pupil begins by sharing their dream for the world for the next 50 years. (An example is given in the item 'Community aims for a new century' on page 151.)

Five other young people (aged between 15 and 25) lead the assembly in Intercessions on the following topics:
• For help to be positive at the start of a new millennium.
• For a sense of responsibility for one another.
• For tolerance towards differences in our society.

- For those feeling afraid and depressed.
- For the guidance of the Holy Spirit for our leaders and for ourselves in our day-to-day decisions.

At the end of the Intercessions a Taizé chant or a meditative song is sung to introduce a period of *deep silence* (lasting at least one full minute), during which each worshipper offers their will to God for the future of society. Suitable chants/songs are: 'Veni Sancte Spiritus'; 'Ubi Caritas'; 'Christe Domine Jesu'; 'Be still and know that I am God'; 'God be in my head, and in my understanding'.

Worship Leader 4 leads the assembly in saying or singing the *Lord's Prayer*. It should be said in the different languages spoken by the various groups in the assembly. Such use can be achieved by each person saying the prayer simultaneously in their own language, or by the assembly saying or singing the prayer in each of the official languages of the country. Taizé Chant No. 93 also shows how the Lord's Prayer can be sung using many languages at the same time to the same chant.

At the end of the Prayer *silence* should be kept for a period, supported if necessary by music played quietly.

Commitment for the future

All the assembly stands, while *a child* (or a small group of children) leads them in this act of Commitment, in which the people's responses are printed in bold type:

To God we give our lives;
In Christ we live for others.
In the Spirit we will work for peace;
With God's *shalom* bring wholeness to the world.
In those in need we will look for Christ,
and minister as servants of the Lord.
We will grow flowers in God's garden,
And share this Universe with all God's creatures.
We will respect the cultures of our neighbours,
and build up the global community with love.
We will light the candle of hope for the depressed,
and protect the innocent from the abuser.

We will rejoice at the discoveries of humanity,
and act responsibly for the welfare of all.
We will uphold the world in prayer,
and draw strength from God for our common journey.
To God be all praise and glory,
for ever and ever, to the end of all ages.
Amen.

A *Collection* shall then be gathered – of food or clothing for those in need locally, or of money for distribution to a development project further away. Those planning the service should make a decision as to how the Collection is to be distributed and should clearly indicate this in the publicity prior to the service.

A drama or video may be displayed while the Collection is gathered. A dance may be used to accompany the offering of the Collection. A worship leader may make a prayer over the offering.

Peace, blessing and dismissal

The assembly stands while one of the oldest members among them comes forward to share the *Peace*, saying:

As I have experienced God's peace throughout the [*number*] years of my long life, so I share it with you all. May the peace of God be among us.

The people reply:

God keep you in perfect peace.

The Peace is then shared among everyone in the assembly, while suitable music is played.

The assembly may then kneel or sit for the *Blessing*, which is given by one of the senior worship leaders, who says:

Our peace comes from God's blessing;
let us be still and wait upon the Lord. (*Pause*.)
May the God of Abraham and Sarah,
May the God of Mary and Joseph,
May the God who shared our humanity,

and breathed into us eternal life,
Bless you, and guide you,
Protect you, and uphold you,
In the power of the Holy Spirit,
And in the love of Jesus Christ,
this day and for ever and ever.

To which the people respond firmly:

Amen and amen.

The assembly concludes the worship by singing a *Hymn or Song*, before being dismissed by a young child. Suggested hymns are those not used earlier from the collection written for the new millennium on pages 175–201, and 'We are marching'; 'God of the ages, by whose hand'; 'The journey of life may be easy, may be hard'.

A child then uses this *Dismissal*, the people making the responses in bold type:

I stand at the beginning of my new life.
We stand on the threshold of a new millennium.
Go forth in hope, in truth, and in love.
We go to serve the Prince of Peace.
Then go in the name of Jesus Christ;
We will go in the power of his Holy Spirit.
(*Together:*) **God bless us all.**

As joyful music is played, the child, the oldest person and the senior worship leader are led out of the assembly by the dancers, to be followed by all the people.

So ends the worship, which should be followed by a time of fellowship and mutual greeting.

THE FEAST OF THE ASCENSION (1 JUNE 2000)

The gathering

The various representatives of the Christian communities in the area are invited to bring an important symbol of God's love and power for them, and place this symbol reverently in an allotted space in the worship area. As the people gather, it is recommended that the various cultural groups sit together so that they are clearly identified in the assembly.

A representative group of Christian leaders should be seated so as to be visible to the people, but without obscuring any of the worship symbols. If possible they should be so seated as to be able to see the Ascension focus.

This focus should be set up at the front of the worship space. A suggested design consists of a long drape of material, affixed at ceiling height and stretching to the floor. At the foot there is placed a floral arrangement in the shape of a rounded hill. In the centre, to represent the Christ at Ascension there is a column of flowers in white and with some red flowers added as a sign of the mark of the nails on the hands and feet. Around the base of the column are arranged a mass of different coloured flowers, representing the disciples of every generation and race. The arrangement needs to be large enough to be seen clearly from the centre of the worship space as a whole.

The paschal candle should be placed on a stand beside the Ascension symbol so that the height of the flame is level with the column of flowers. It should be lit at the beginning of the service. Incense and a burner should be prepared for use during the service in association with the symbol.

It is recommended that the material should be of natural or white colour, and the top be so arranged that it is able to receive a projected image of coloured segments to represent the glory of heaven at the appropriate time as indicated below.

In those parts of the worship space which are furthest from the Ascension focus there should be additional displays of flowers and candles. In these areas some of the symbols presented to the assembly by the cultural groups will also be displayed.

A stand, from which the Scriptures will be read, should be placed in the centre of the floor area of the worship space at a height to be clearly visible to all those gathered. It should be focused by lighting so as to make it a significant symbol. The Scriptures should be placed on the stand. A microphone should relay the sound of the readings to all parts of the worship area. Further microphones should be available for the President of the worship, for the other worship leaders, for the intercessors, for the children and young people's groups, and for the musical groups and soloists. Adequate sound amplification equipment will be required.

While the people are assembling choirs should sing, quietly in their own language, songs preparing the people for worship. If there are over 1000 people expected for the service it may be necessary to add instrumental or taped music to cover the time taken to gather the people.

When all the people have assembled a church leader chosen to preside at the worship should welcome the various Christian communities, the representatives of the wider community and those people of other faiths.

Call to worship

The President's words of welcome shall conclude with this call to worship:

Let us lift our hearts to heaven in joyful expectation of God's presence with us. Let us praise God for the past, the present and the future as we celebrate the year 2000.

We recall the wonder of the Incarnation of God in Christ, who took upon himself our humanity and suffered pain and death like us.

We affirm our faith that this Christ was raised from the dead and ascended into heaven to assume all power and responsibility for our world.

We attest our experience that the Holy Spirit has come among us to comfort and strengthen us for our work as disciples of Christ.

We acknowledge God's presence with us now, renewing and reconciling us as one body in Christ.

We trust God for our future and that of the world, believing that God's love and purpose is for the welfare of us all.

Through our baptism we have experienced God's love for us and our call to worship, witness and service.

So let us fulfil our calling as Christ's disciples and offer our hearts and lives to God in this service of praise, adoration and commitment.

Worship Leader 1 says:

Lift up your voices. Let us sing to the Lord our Creator.

The Cantors and People sing in chorus: 'Let us sing to the Lord our creator' (Taizé Chant No. 26, *'Bénissez le Seigneur!'*) or 'Praise the Lord, ye heavens adore him' (*With One Voice*, No. 58).

Worship Leader 1 says, with affirming response from all the people:

Jesus, our ascended and exalted Lord,
to whom has been given the name above all names;
we worship and adore you.
Jesus, King of righteousness, King of peace,

enthroned at the right hand of the majesty on high;
we worship and adore you.
Jesus, our great High Priest, our Advocate with the Father;
who lives for ever to make intercession for us;
we worship and adore you.
Jesus, the Pioneer of our salvation,
bringing many to glory through your Passion;
we worship and adore you.
'To him who sits on the throne and to the Lamb,
be praise and honour and glory and power for ever and ever';
Amen. We praise and honour you.
Eternal God,
you have given your Son authority in heaven and in earth,
grant that we may never lose the vision of his Kingdom,
but worship and serve him with hope and joy,
for he reigns with you and the Holy Spirit, one God eternally.
Amen.

The assembly is seated as a choir of children sings this hymn (*100 Hymns for Today*, No. 98, or *With One Voice*, No. 189):

We have a gospel to proclaim,
good news for folk in all the earth;
the gospel of a Saviour's name:
we sing his glory, tell his worth.

Worship Leader 2 reads Psalm 47, with the People making this refrain at the end of verses 1, 4, 8 and 10:

God ascends to the throne with shouts of joy.

At the conclusion of the Psalm a group of instrumentalists plays a musical piece as the incense is made ready and a procession approaches the paschal candle and the symbol of the Ascension. When all are in place Reader 1 reads the account of the Ascension:

The record of Christ's Ascension from the Acts of the Apostles, chapter 1, beginning at verse 1. (*Read Acts 1:1–11.*)

As the Scripture is read, at the appropriate place, the paschal candle is extinguished to show that the resurrection appearances are at an end. The incense is lit to allow billows of clouds to cover the floral symbol. The projection of multicoloured lights shines from the top of the fabric to represent the heavenly welcome to the Ascended Christ.

The congregation stand to sing the Hymn: 'Come let us with our Lord arise' (*With One Voice*, No. 297) or 'Hail the day that sees him rise' (*With One Voice*, No. 291).

Reader 2 reads the Epistle (Ephesians 1:15–23):

The Epistle to the Ephesians, chapter 1, reading from verse 15. This passage begins with a prayer for the hearers, and ends with an affirmation of the power of Christ, seated at God's right hand.

The congregation responds with the Hymn 'New age is dawning' (see page 182) or Taizé Chant No. 19, '*Laudate omnes gentes*':

Sing praises all you people.
Sing praises to the Lord.

Or this chorus and refrain (*With One Voice*, No. 674):

Alleluia, alleluia, give thanks to the risen Lord,
alleluia, alleluia, give praise to his name.

Jesus is Lord of all the earth,
he is the King of creation.

Spread the good news to all the earth,
Jesus has died and has risen.

We have been crucified with Christ;
now we shall live for ever.

Come let us praise the living God,
joyfully sing to our Saviour.

The assembly turns to face the centre of the worship area to listen to the Gospel. They may stand or sit, as is thought best for sight and hearing. Reader 3 reads the Gospel (Matthew 28:16–20):

The Gospel according to St Matthew, chapter 28, reading from verse 16: 'Christ's authority and command'.

A *Fanfare* notes the end of the reading, and then there is time for Reflection. This is supported by the playing of quiet music on an instrument or tape. The assembly is seated.

Worship Leader 3 concludes the Reflection time with this prayer:

> Our Father in heaven, help us to keep in mind
> that Christ our Saviour lives with you in glory,
> and yet promised to remain with us until the end of time;
> keep us always joyful and expectant in worship and service,
> for you are our God for ever and ever.
> Amen.

Then all the members of the assembly are invited to say or sing the *Lord's Prayer* in their own language. A group of at least three people, using different languages simultaneously, should model this with the assistance of the sound system.

The President shall then introduce *Three Speakers*. The speakers are invited to give testimony to the meaning of the year 2000 for them in their Christian faith and service. Each speaker can be supported by a short song from their cultural group at the end of the address.

A group of young women and men shall lead the assembly in an act of responsive praise to the Ascended Christ, saying:

> *Men:*   Glory to our ascended Lord,
> **for he is with us always.**
> *Women:* Glory to the Word of God,
> **going forth to make disciples in every nation.**
> *Men:*   Glory to Christ,
> **who has given gifts for the perfecting of the Saints.**
> *Women:* Glory to our High Priest,
> **who intercedes for us and all people.**
> *Men:*   Glory to our Pioneer,
> **who has journeyed to heaven**
> **to prepare a place for us.**
> *Women:* Glory to Jesus, the author and finisher of our faith,
> **who has promised to come again**
> **to bring to completion all of Creation.**

Men: Glory to you, our Ascended Christ,
          for you live and reign with the Father and the Spirit,
All: **one God for evermore. Amen.**

The assembly is invited to sit or kneel to join in this Taizé Chant:

Jesus, remember me when you come into your kingdom.

Or use other similar music which prepares the people to enter a period of *deep silence* for several minutes.

At the conclusion of the Silence a choir (with the people if desired) will sing a form of *Kyrie Eleison* (e.g. Taizé Chants No. 84–86, 88–90 or other settings known locally).

The President then stands and reads this *Sentence* from Scripture (John 14:27a):

Peace I leave with you. My peace I give to you.

After a silent pause, the President invites the whole assembly to rise and share the *Peace* as an act of reconciliation and unity.

After the Peace has been widely shared, it is suggested that some music is played to re-focus the congregation. During the playing of the music the incense is brought to the centre of the worship space, where it is lit in a large bowl so that clouds of incense begin to rise in preparation for the Intercessions.

Worship Leader 4 invites the assembly to prepare for the Intercessions, and then reads this Scripture Sentence (Hebrews 4:14–16):

Since, then, we have a great high priest who has passed through the heavens, Jesus the Son of God, let us hold fast to our confession. For we do not have a high priest who is unable to sympathize with our weakness, but we have one who in every respect has been tested as we are, yet without sin. Let us therefore approach the throne of grace with boldness, so that we may receive mercy and find grace to help in time of need.
Alleluia, we come with Christ.

The Intercessions

These are led by a group representative of age, gender and culture. The Intercessions should acknowledge that Christ prays with us and for us, and understands our human condition. The Intercessions should be focused on our need for reconciliation and harmony; our request for empowerment to respond to the needs of the weak and broken among us; our commitment to outreach and mission in the power of the Spirit; and our responsibilities as citizens of our countries.

A sung or said response by the people should affirm each part of the Intercessions. At the end of the Intercessions the President leads the assembly in saying together the *Grace*.

The assembly sings a *Hymn or Song* celebrating the new millennium, such as those found on pages 175–201.

The Blessing

Worship Leader 5 reads this collect prayer:

>Eternal God, bless us now with your love and power
>as your Son our Lord blessed his disciples at his Ascension;
>help us to take your Gospel into all the world
>and to live the Good News we proclaim;
>let the Spirit's power give us new energy for the new millennium,
>so that our lives praise you, O God, Father, Son and Holy Spirit.
>**Amen.**

It is suggested that some quiet music be played while a group of six elderly persons and six children aged eight to ten come forward as representatives of all to be blessed by the President, who then turns to bless the whole assembly with these words:

>The peace of God keep you safe.
>The power of God strengthen your lives in all goodness.
>The guiding hand of God lead you in your journey to heaven
>to discover the welcome of Christ's embrace.
>May the One God in Trinity,
>the Father, the Son and the Holy Spirit,
>who created us, redeemed us, and gives us life,

bless each one,
now and always.
(The People with a loud voice respond:) **Amen**.

A young child shall then dismiss the assembly with these words:

Go forth as Christ's disciples.

To which the people respond:

We will go in the name of Christ.

A *Dismissal Hymn or Chorus* shall be sung by the assembly. Suggested music includes: 'It all depends' (page 186); 'Lead us, heavenly Father, lead us' (*With One Voice*, No. 492); 'Guide me, O thou great Jehovah' (*With One Voice*, No. 478); 'Jubilate Deo, jubilate Deo, alleluia' (Taizé Chant No. 31).

The Hymn concluded, music will continue to allow the assembly to mingle with one another and view with reverence the symbols brought by the various groups.

A SERVICE OF THE SPIRIT: 'INTO THE FUTURE'

The date

It is suggested that this service might be held at the turn of the year, on 31 December/ 1 January. It could be a 'Watch Night Service', following the traditions of many people whose homeland is Scotland. Such a service takes place on the last day of the year late at night so that at midnight the new year is welcomed with rejoicing and prayers for strength and guidance. Such a service could also be held on the first day of the new year at some suitable time during that day. Clearly, the years 2000 and 2001 have a double significance as the beginning of both a new century and a new millennium.

The theme

The service has the title 'Into the future', with a theme of recalling and redeeming the past, and entering into the future. In accordance with this theme it begins with a thanksgiving for all that has shaped the present day, and concludes with prayers for strength to face the future and to achieve the goals of harmony with nature and with all of humanity.

The participants

It is suggested that the Christian ecumenical community takes the lead in inviting those of other faiths, and all those from the wider community who are willing to join in such a 'service of the spirit'. The invitation should make it clear that the whole community is invited, and declare the purpose of the service.

The setting

The setting may reflect this community emphasis, and the service may be held in a large community theatre or a town hall or an open park or stadium. Symbols of the relevant community (national/ regional/ city-wide) should be prominently displayed. These could be flags, posters, national symbols and cultural treasures. It may be advisable to use a stage or raised podium on which the leading representatives of the community are asked to gather, each wearing the dress appropriate to their office. Cultural and religious diversity should be obvious from the setting.

The assembly should be arranged to establish a unity, placing the seating to allow for the opportunity during the service to greet others who are sharing in this occasion. If the setting is outside, care should be taken to provide sound amplification and, if possible, big-screen technology for the projection of images.

Leadership

The leadership of the service will include community leaders, representatives of the various religious bodies, a group of children, massed choirs, a children's choir, and a band or orchestra.

The welcome and gathering

A community leader (e.g. the head of state or the elected head of government at a national event) should welcome the assembly and introduce the national anthem or some other appropriate song known to the assembly. The community leader then invites all members of the assembly to greet those around them with the cultural form of mutual greeting. During this activity a band or orchestra plays suitable music. The assembly members are encouraged to greet those whom they do not know as well as their friends. Sufficient time will be allowed for this activity.

Acknowledgement of the Spirit

Worship Leader 1 calls on the assembly to acknowledge that the Spirit of God gives value, vision, hope and strength to the community. The people respond in words of faith and affirmation (printed in bold type):

Before we came into being, there was a Creation;
Before we awoke, there was a world;
Before we existed, there was a past;
After we have ceased to be, there will be a future.
Spirit of God, inspire your Creation;
Breathe new life into our community;
And bind us to yourself and to one another.

Before we give form to an idea, there is a spirit of inspiration;
Before we implement a vision, there is a spirit of strength;
Before we bring our plans to fruition, there is a spirit of purpose;
When all is complete, there is a spirit of joy.
Spirit of God, guide our future;
Enlarge our vision;
Shape our plans;
And rejoice with us in our achievements.

Before we despoil our environment, there is still a spirit of recovery;
Before we exhaust our earth, there is still a spirit of restraint;
Before we annihilate our enemies, there is still a spirit of forgiveness;
When we fear total destruction, there is still a spirit of comfort.
Spirit of God, restrain our greed;
Turn our hearts to justice;
Call us to forgiveness;
And sustain our hopes for peace.

Come, Spirit of God, come among us.
Open our hearts to acknowledge your presence.

A massed choir (or the whole assembly) responds with a song. Suitable songs are: Beethoven's 'Ode to Joy' (the finale of the Ninth Symphony); Haydn's 'Creation's Hymn' ('The heavens are telling'); the Taizé Chant *'Veni Creator Spiritus'*; and for a Christian community, 'O Lord of every shining constellation' or 'Filled with the Spirit's power, with one accord'.

Treasuring the past with thanksgiving

Worship Leader 2 says to the assembly:

Kenneth Clark, speaking about civilization, had this wisdom to share, using the word 'man' to include all of us: 'Civilized man, or so it seems to me, must feel he belongs somewhere in space and time, that he consciously looks forward and looks back.'[1]

Let us join together in reflecting on our past, giving thanks for the achievements of our ancestors, in both material and spiritual things. Let us also note human failure and the evil that has also come from the heart of humanity, so that we learn the lessons from failure and turn away from evil. Only then is it right that we should rejoice at the gifts of today and face the future with hope.

Reader 1 says:

Kenneth Clark also wrote: 'There have been times in history when the earth seems suddenly to have grown warmer or more radio-active... I don't put that forward as a scientific proposition, but the fact remains that three or four times in history *humanity* has made a great leap forward that would have been unthinkable under ordinary evolutionary conditions. One such time was about the year 3000 BC, when quite suddenly civilization appeared, not only in Egypt and Mesopotamia but in the Indus valley; another was in the late sixth century BC, when there was not only the miracle of Ionia and Greece – philosophy, science, art, poetry, all reaching a point that wasn't reached again for 2000 years – but also in India a spiritual enlighten-ment that has perhaps never been equalled. Another was around the year 1100. It seems to have affected the whole world; but its strongest and most dramatic effect was in Western Europe – where it was most needed. It was like a Russian spring. In every branch of life – action, philosophy, organization, technology – there was an extra-ordinary outpouring of energy, an intensification of existence... The evidence of this heroic energy, this confidence, this strength of will and intellect, is still visible to us.'[2]

Worship Leader 2 leads the assembly in an act of thanksgiving:

Let us give thanks for the gifts given to humanity
over many millennia, and for our ancestors

who have brought them to fruition for us to enjoy.
For the gifts of artists, poets, composers and writers;
of architects, designers, engineers and planners;
of builders, publishers, carvers and producers;
We give thanks for the inheritance of the past.

For technology and communication,
which bring us closer together;
for the discoveries of medicine and developments in surgery,
which sustain our health;
for the understanding of the processes of the mind and the psyche,
through which we bind up the wounds of the spirit;
We give thanks for the inheritance of the past.

For the treasures of education and experience;
for the accumulation of knowledge of how things work;
for explorations beyond the boundaries of the known;
We give thanks for the inheritance of the past.

For the cultivation and conservation of the resources of nature;
for the highways and airways and all the means of transportation;
for the systems of government and patterns of trade;
We give thanks for the inheritance of the past.

For those who have stood for justice and peace;
for those who have sacrificed their lives that others may live;
for those who sustained hope when disaster descended;
We give thanks for the heroes and heroines of the past.

Reader 2 reads from the Book of Ecclesiasticus:

Let us now sing the praises of the famous, our ancestors in their generations... These were those who ruled in their kingdoms, and made a name for themselves by their valour; those who gave counsel because they were intelligent; those who spoke in prophetic oracles; those who led the people by their counsels and by their knowledge of the people's lore; they were wise in their instruction; those who composed musical tunes, and put verses in writing; the rich endowed with resources, living peacefully in their homes – all these were honoured in their generations, and were the pride of their times. Some of them left behind a name so that others may declare their praise. But of others there is no memory ... though they were also godly, whose righteous deeds have not been forgotten... The name of all these men and women lives on generation after generation. The assembly declares their wisdom, and the congregation proclaims their praise.[3]

A song of thanksgiving is sung by the assembly, led by the massed choirs. During the singing of the song a cluster of candles is lit as a sign of thankful remembrance for the past. Suitable songs are: 'Thank you for giving me the morning' (verses 1–4 only); 'All creatures of our God and King' (verses 1–5 only); the Taizé Chants 'Bless the Lord', *'Laudate Domine'* and *'Jubilate Deo'*; music from religious traditions among the assembly.

Turning away from evil

Worship Leader 3 speaks to the people:

Dag Hammarskjöld, a former Secretary General of the United Nations, gave us this advice: 'You cannot play with the animal in you without becoming wholly animal, play with falsehood without forfeiting your right to the truth, play with cruelty without losing your sensitivity of mind. He who wants to keep his garden tidy, doesn't reserve a plot for weeds.'[4]

So let us examine with humility the failures of the past and the evils done by ourselves and our predecessors. Let us face the truth so that we can turn away from evil and find a better way for the future. The truth hurts most when we look such evil in the face, and name it for the wickedness that it is. We must own our part in its destruction, and resolve to heal the pain with love. Let us use this meditation to strengthen our resolve to take our part in such healing. (*Projected images should be used to illustrate the various parts of the following meditation.*)

That face has haunted me. It is a living reproach,
a prolonged cry that reaches me in my seclusion.
That face is young, but human sin has struck it hard.
It was defenceless and exposed to every blow.

From every side those blows came –

Destitution:
    the shanty dwelling,
    the dilapidated bed,

the foul air,
smoke,
alcohol,
drugs,
hunger,
hospital,
prison,
work – once there was work –
    crushing, humiliating, degrading;
then unemployment,
depression and war.

Diversion:
    frenzied dances,
    revolting songs,
    demoralizing films,
    langorous music,
    unclean and deceitful kisses.

Violence:
    the push and shove to gain a living,
    rebellion,
    brawls,
    cries,
    blows,
    hate,
    rape.

The people of evil came from everywhere,
men and women with their horrid selfishness,
their dreadful faces, their great, dirty, grasping fingers,
their broken nails, their fetid breath.
From the ends of the earth, from the bounds of time, they come,
slowly one at a time, or suddenly all together like brutes,
    striking,
    whipping,
    lashing,
    hammering,
    this poor face.
It took eighteen years to fashion it,

hundreds of centuries to produce it,
    the poor face of this child of man.

To look at this face is to look into an open book
of the miseries and the sins of us all –
of selfishness, conceit, cowardice,
    of greed, lust, abdications, compromises.
Yet in this twisted face are the eyes of tragic supplication –
the infinite desire of a soul to live above its mud.

Oh God! that face haunts me, it frightens me, it condemns me;
for with everyone else I have caused it or allowed it to become like
    that.
And I realize that this face is the face of one of my brothers and
    sisters.
What have we done to another member of the family?[5]

After a pause the assembly responds:

Help us to forgive and be forgiven.
Help us to turn away from evil.
May love restore the twisted face in us all.

A solo singer (or a recorded voice) affirms the words with a song of love
and hope. An example of such a song is 'Love changes everything' from
Aspects of Love.[6]

As the song comes to an end Worship Leader 3 symbolically washes the
face of a young person which has been streaked with the grime of oppression and the tears of pain, to restore a look of value and contentment. In a
large assembly this action should be projected onto the screen. At the end
of the symbolic action Worship Leader 3 invites the people to stand and
respond:

We will forgive one another, and receive forgiveness.
We will turn away from evil.
We will overcome evil with love.
Spirit of God, strengthen our resolve for good.

The assembly is seated again.

Living life now

Worship Leader 4 says:

> Here are some words of Mother Teresa of Calcutta 'On Kindness': 'Be kind and merciful. Let no one ever come to you without coming away better and happier. Be the living expression of God's kindness: kindness in your face, kindness in your eyes, kindness in your smile, kindness in your warm greeting. In the slums we are the light of God's kindness to the poor. To children, to the poor, to all who suffer and are lonely, give always a happy smile – give them not only your care, but also your heart.'[7]

Worship Leader 4 invites representatives of four organizations providing care within the community briefly to address the assembly with examples of how they are caring for those with a variety of needs. (These addresses may be illustrated on the screen during their delivery.)

After the conclusion of the last address a choir of children sings a song about kindness according to one of the cultures of the nation/region. A suitable song called 'Kindness' is provided by a New Zealand composer on page 188.

Worship Leader 4 leads the assembly in this act of affirmation:

> When I was hungry, you gave me to eat,
> **When I was thirsty, you gave me a drink.**
> When I was homeless, you opened your doors,
> **When I was naked, you gave me your coat.**
> When I was weary, you helped me find rest,
> **When I was anxious, you calmed all my fears.**
> When I was little, you taught me to read,
> **When I was lonely, you gave me your love.**
> When in a prison, you came to my cell,
> **When on a sick bed, you cared for my needs.**
> In a strange country, you made me at home,
> **Seeking employment, you found me a job.**
> Hurt in a battle, you bound up my wounds,
> **Searching for kindness, you held out your hand.**
> When I was Coloured, an Outsider, or White,
> **Mocked and insulted, you carried my cross.**

When I was agèd, you bothered to smile,
When I was restless, you listened and cared.
You saw me covered in spittle and blood,
You knew my features, though grimy with sweat.
When I was laughed at, you stood by my side,
When I was happy, you shared in my joy.[8]

Thank you my neighbour, thank you my friend,
We'll share together 'til life shall end.

Facing the future with hope

At this point of the service it is suggested that a peal of bells be rung, both inside the assembly building and across the city from all those civic and church buildings that have a peal of bells. In other cultures the appropriate sound of joy may be from a horn, a drum or a gong. At a midnight service this sound should go forth as the clock turns from one year to the next.

Worship Leader 5 reads these sayings of Dag Hammarskjöld:

I am being driven forward
into an unknown land.
The pass grows steeper,
the air colder and sharper.
A mind from an unknown goal
stirs the strings
of expectation.
   Still the question:
   Shall I ever get there?
   There where life resounds
   a clear pure note
   in the silence.

And

Never look down to test the ground before taking your next step;
only *the one* who keeps *the* eye fixed on the far horizon,
will find *the* right road.
Never measure the height of a mountain,
until you have reached the top.
Then you will see how low it is.[9]

One of the leaders from the various faith communities is invited to deliver a *Message of Hope* for the future.

If there is agreement by the representatives of the faith communities, the address may be followed by the reading of Psalm 46 from the Hebrew Scriptures. Alternatively, a choir or solo item is suggested, using suitable music for the theme of hope. An example of such a solo would be 'Climb Ev'ry Mountain' from Rodgers' and Hammerstein's show *The Sound of Music*.

Children are invited to come forward to lead the assembly in this Prayer of Hope, to which the people respond:

Divine Spirit,
Guide us on our pathway into the future.
Give us strength when we grow weary from the journey.
Encourage us when the light of hope burns low.
Inspire us to give each other a helping hand along the way.

Create in us a new spirit to act with kindness and to speak the truth.
Bring us together in harmony to find the road to peace.
Come, Divine Spirit, unite us as one.
Help us to care for the Creation
and for all living things who share our Universe.
Implant in our hearts loving respect for all the peoples of the world.
Come, Divine Spirit, touch our lives with your fullness.

The assembly will then stand and move to join hands with one another while the massed choirs and soloists sing a song of unity such as *'Amigos Para Siempre'* ('Friends for Life', the official theme of the 1992 Barcelona Olympic Games) or 'The Children's Song' (from the opening of the 1998 Winter Olympics at Nagano, Japan). If necessary these songs can be played from tape or video recordings.

The assembly disperses slowly, allowing time to talk with those they meet. It is suggested that the band or orchestra continues to play the final song tune for some time while the people leave.

8

THEMES, READINGS
AND PRAYERS FOR
CONGREGATIONAL
WORSHIP

These themes, readings and prayers are provided to assist those planning worship within local congregations to mark the start of a new millennium. They will find here a set of themes which sum up our thoughts as we enter this new period of the history of humanity. Under each theme I have provided a set of readings from the Holy Scriptures. These give the planners a choice of readings to fit into the regular pattern of their weekly worship. They could also be used for a service of six progressive lessons from Scripture interspersed with suitable music, reflections by members of the congregation on the theme, readings from the selections in Chapter 10, 'Messages for a New Millennium', and some of the prayers which follow later in this chapter.

Planning groups should look carefully at the material in Chapter 7, 'Outlines of Services for Public Worship', to see what material is provided there which would be suitable for use at a congregational level. They will be able to glean many useful ideas of ways to involve the local congregation in dance and drama, and the creation of symbols for their worship. Use of this material will also link them with the regional and national events. It is suggested that during the local congregational celebration links should be made with the regional and national events by repeating the use of key symbols, showing sections of the public worship on video, or receiving reports from representatives of the local congregation who attended the wider events.

I am sure that those who are responsible for planning congregational worship will have in mind the note of inclusiveness as to gender, age, race and culture. It would also be good if they were able to establish links with at least one other congregation across the globe who would provide them with a different perspective and help them to see the worldwide nature of these celebrations.

In addition to using one or more of these thematic services during the year, I suggest that the regular use of a collect for 'Worship 2000' within the usual services would help us all to remember the significance of the year for Christians. It would also help members of the congregation to seek out opportunities for witness to Jesus Christ among those with whom they live and work. Examples for such a collect are to be found below. Those who lead intercessions may also like to have the key themes for this year in mind as they lead the prayers of the people week by week. There are plenty of prayers set out below, and these can be used in the form in which they are printed or they can be adapted to suit the local custom and language for prayer. Within the themes there is a need to focus particularly on our responsibility for the care of Creation, for the nurture of the new generation of children and young people, for vision and accountability in our leaders, and for a strong sense of participation of all people in the formation of a world more in tune with God's will.

SUITABLE THEMES FOR THE YEAR 2000

1. Living life in thanksgiving to God.
2. Celebrating the Incarnation of Jesus Christ.
3. Rejoicing in the rule of God and the companionship of Christ.
4. Making the most of this time.
5. Living in hope.
6. A world in harmony – God's call and our responsibility.
7. Partners in prayer and work.

BIBLE READINGS ON EACH THEME

1. Living life in thanksgiving to God

1 Chronicles 16:8–15: David's Psalm of thanksgiving.
Psalm 145:10–21: All your works shall give thanks to you, O Lord.
Mark 8:1–10: Giving thanks, he broke the bread.
2 Corinthians 4:13–18: Living by faith with thanksgiving.
2 Corinthians 9:8–15: God's generosity is for sharing with thanksgiving.

Ephesians 5:15–20: Living carefully, giving thanks to God.
Philippians 4:4–9: Giving thanks in prayer, and doing what is right.
Colossians 2:6–10: Living life to the full with thanksgiving.

2. Celebrating the Incarnation of Christ

See the readings suggested in the Epiphany Service for Public Worship (page 97).

3. Rejoicing in the rule of God and the companionship of Christ

See the readings suggested in the Ascension Service for Public Worship (page 105).

4. Making the most of this time

Psalm 34:1–15: Bless the Lord at all times.
Isaiah 49:8–13: God's new time.
Isaiah 60:19–22: God's time of light.
Ezekiel 7:5–12: A time of judgement.
Zephaniah 3:8–13: A time of God's redemption.
Mark 1:9–14: The time is fulfilled.
Romans 13:11–14: Urgent times.
2 Corinthians 6:1–10: Now is the acceptable time.
Colossians 4:2–6: Making the most of the time.
Revelation 1:4–8: The Alpha and the Omega.

5. Living in hope

Psalm 42: A song of hope and trust.
Proverbs 24:13–14: Our hope lies in wisdom.
Jeremiah 31:15–17: Hope for the future return of our children.
Luke 12:22–31: Do not be anxious.
Romans 5:1–5: Hope does not disappoint us.
Romans 15:13: A blessing of hope.
1 Thessalonians 5:1–11: Hope, the helmet of salvation.
1 Peter 1:3–9: A living hope.

6. A world in harmony – God's call and our responsibility

Numbers 6:22–26: A blessing of peace.
Psalm 122: A prayer for peace.
Isaiah 9:2–7: The Prince of Peace.
Isaiah 32:16–18: Righteousness and peace.
John 14:25–29: The promise of peace.
John 20: 19–23: Peace be with you.
Romans 12:14–21: Live in harmony.
Romans 15:1–6: Please others, not yourselves.
1 Corinthians 13:4–13: The greatest gift is love.
1 Thessalonians 5:12–23: Be at peace among yourselves.
1 John 3:11–17 (or 11–24): Love one another.

7. Partners in prayer and work

Psalm 5: Lord, hear my prayer as I worship.
Isaiah 56:1–3a, 6–7: A house of prayer for all people.
Luke 11:5–13: Perseverance in prayer.
2 Corinthians 1:8–11: Prayer in aid of the afflicted.
1 Thessalonians 3:12–13: A prayer for love and holiness.
1 Timothy 2:1–7: Instructions concerning prayer.
1 Peter 3:8–12: God's ears are open to our prayers.

PRAYERS FOR CONGREGATIONAL WORSHIP

Collects for Worship 2000

God of new beginnings,
  we thank you for the birth of Jesus, your Son,
  by which we mark the start of a new era in human history.
Help us by your Spirit to celebrate the fact
  that you shared our human experience
  and understand us from the inside.
In this year 2000 give us thankfulness for the past,
  strength for the present, and vision for the future.
Make us more aware of the needs of ourselves
  and those who share our world,
  then give us the mind and heart to find ways to meet those needs.
Let your Spirit energize our prayers and our actions,

so that this 'Amen' is the pledge of our full commitment,
for the love of Jesus our Saviour.
Amen.

Or:

God, our God, you are the same yesterday, today and for ever.
We thank you for the certainty of your love,
strength, forgiveness and hope,
year in and year out.
We pray for our generation as it begins a new millennium.
May we treasure the good things of the past,
and not turn our backs on them because they are 'old'.
May we forgive the hurts of one another, and turn from hatred
to loving respect for those who differ from us.
May we discern what is just and true,
and promote the welfare of everyone
in our community and our world.
Above all, may we witness to the joy of your Gospel,
and serve you in our care of one another.
So we will honour you, our God,
and praise your name for ever and ever.
Amen.

Prayers for each theme

1. *Living life in thanksgiving to God*
A THANKSGIVING
Creator God, thank you
for the beautiful world we enjoy,
for its herds of animals and plants and flowers,
and for all that is good and wonderful;
for the air we breathe and the food we eat,
for our friends, our family and everyone else
who cherishes and cares for us.
But, dear God,
help us not to take all this for granted,
and, as we come to the end of this century,
make us grateful for what we have.
May we remember those who are less fortunate than we are,
and turn away from being wasteful or greedy,

ever being content and happy
  in your endless love and goodness.
Thanks be to you, Our Lord and Our God.
Amen.
(Arul Thavarajah, King's College)

A CHILDREN'S THANKSGIVING
God, our Creator and our Friend
Your listening ear to us bend.
Thanks for all the stuff you have made,
for Jesus Christ and the price he paid.
Thank you too for the food we eat,
and the beauty of the fields of wheat.
We appreciate all you've done,
the sky and stars, and moon and sun.
Thank you, God, for all your Creation,
and the promise of the next generation.
Help us all to shine as lights for you,
lead and guide us in all we do.
Forgive our sins and all that's past,
cleaning up your Creation fast.
For the love of Christ we pray,
listen and hear our prayer today.
Amen.
(Miriam Bissett, Fiora Au, Sarah Allerby and Violet Kua,
Diocesan School)

2. *Celebrating the Incarnation of Jesus Christ*
TEACH US HOW TO LIVE
Gracious God,
    Thank you for letting humanity survive
        for so long in this world
    which you have created.
    Thank you for sending your Son, Jesus Christ,
        to teach and show us how to live.
In this new millennium help us to strive
    to right all of our wrongs,
        to create equality among all your creatures,
    and, most of all,
        to learn to love you more and more,

and live as Jesus taught us
in the power of your Holy Spirit.
Amen.

(G. Rhodes, King's College)

THE WAY OF THE CROSS

Lord Jesus,
when our cross is heavy,
when life is hard,
and we do not know the way,
then, walk with us,
stay with us,
that we may accept our difficulties,
knowing that your presence and your love are with us,
always.
Amen.

(Rosemary Atkins)

OUR LEADER

Jesus, we thank you,
that you lead us through times of trouble,
when the darkness surrounds our lives;
that you help us to seek your light,
when the path before us is dark.
Jesus, we thank you,
that you taught us to accept you and others into our lives,
when all we wanted was to be left alone;
that you and they supported us,
and helped us in our time of need.
Jesus, you showed us the way by sacrificing your own life for all;
help us to understand the significance of what you did for us,
and to follow you, our Leader, in all the days ahead.
Amen.

(Samantha Marsh, Diocesan School)

3. *Rejoicing in the rule of God and the companionship of Christ*

MY COMPANION AND GUIDE

God, my Companion and Guide,
stay near me as I journey in these new years.
Though I have many hard memories of times gone by

let me not fear for the years ahead.
Help me to support new initiatives that give life and hope;
    and in gentle wisdom to have courage to caution
    when your purposes of love and concern are forgotten.
Keep me humble and alive in your Gospel,
    ready to serve where you will lead me.
This I pray in the name of your Son, Jesus Christ,
    my pattern and my guide for all time.
Amen.
(Rosemary Atkins)

HELP US, SAVIOUR

Dear Lord,
In this new generation help us to find our way:
    in difficulties, help us to find resolution;
    in need, help us to find relief,
    in pain, help us to find strength and healing.
When in trouble, help us to find our Saviour;
    when lost, help us to find our path;
    when scared, help us to find our faith;
    when unsure, help us to find you again,
Our Lord and our God.
Amen.
(Andrew Fraser, King's College)

CONSOLATION

Heavenly Father,
    we come to you in the name of Jesus Christ our Lord,
    we acknowledge our need for your comfort and support
    in all that we do in this frantic, technological, ambitious century.
    So we seek your help and guidance in all the decisions we make.
Give us your loving encouragement
    as we face this marvellous millennium.
Heavenly Father,
    thank you for your unfailing loyalty towards us
    in every circumstance of our lives:
    in the times when we have done your will;
    in the times when we have disappointed you,
    and in the times of personal struggles and pain.
Continue to bless us with your acceptance,

>   wise counsel and direction,
> and by your empowering love, give us consolation
>   and your strength for our future,
> in the name of Jesus Christ we pray.
> Amen.

(Aneil Chhima, King's College)

4. *Making the most of this time*

TIME

> On the clock we see the seconds tick away;
>   God, we wonder what we mean when we say,
>   'With you a thousand years is but a day.'
> Each moment is precious and none is wasted with you, my God;
>   things in your world take a long time to mature;
>   help me to have a proper sense of balance over time.
> O my God, make me active in the present,
>   patient for the future,
>   and thankful for the gift of this special moment.

> In this year we call 2000,
>   help me to take seriously the opportunity
>   to begin a new period in human history.
> Let it be a good time when we cooperate to carry the burdens
>   and lighten the loads of our global village.
> Help us redeem this time, making it an occasion
>   for joyful worship and caring service,
>   giving you praise and honour, glory and blessing,
>   for you are our God for ever and ever.
> Amen.

(Peter Atkins)

GOD OF OUR TOMORROWS

> God of Time, of today and of tomorrow,
> thank you for the years I have known,
>   years of unbelievable expansion in knowledge,
>   in space science, in medicine, in technology;
>   years of watching the world become a global village,
>   but sadly also,
>   years of war and violence,
>   of starvation, greed and hatred.

God of our tomorrows, guide me to show
   generosity and care towards those in need,
   peace and friendship to those who differ from me.
May I learn again,
   to worship you, not money,
   to trust you, not warheads,
   to know, through faith in you,
     that peace, hope and love will again reign in your world.
God is in charge of our times.
Alleluia. Amen.

(Rosemary Atkins)

TIME FOR CELEBRATION

God, now is the time for celebration,
   the beginning of a new millennium is upon us,
   and two thousand years after the birth of your Son, Jesus,
   we and countless people praise you still.
Today we ask for your friendship, dear God,
   for if it was not for this,
   our lives which you intended to be full
   would be dismal and empty.
Fill us again with celebration
   as we share our lives with you,
   for you have given us the ability and opportunity to pray
   in the name of your Son, Jesus Christ our Lord.
Amen.

(Shaun Sutton, King's College)

THE BEST IN THE NEW MILLENNIUM

Gracious God,
   As we head into the new millennium,
   help us to find a balance in our lives,
   to accept the changes as they come,
   to retain our values,
   and all that you have taught us.
May we be thankful for what we have,
   strive for what we need,
   and always dream about the best that might yet be.
Give us your Spirit so that each one of us
   may reach our full potential,

and respect one another in love and truth;
    then we will fulfil your hopes for this world,
    today and always.
Amen.
(Shana Chandra and Danielle Evans,
Diocesan School)

5. *Living in hope*

HOPE FOR EACH NEW DAY

God of all,
    thanks for life and living.
Give us courage as we begin this new millennium;
    strength and vitality to proclaim your Gospel;
    love to care where care is needed;
    hope for each new day;
that your kingdom may come on earth,
    and that we may be part of that coming,
in the power of your Holy Spirit,
    and in the name of Jesus Christ, our Saviour.
Amen.
(Peter Atkins)

TRUST

For all of history,
    people have worshipped you, our God;
    people have looked to you for help.
Through all of history,
    you have shown to us your endless love,
    and in you your people trust.
Faithful God,
    in you we have always trusted,
    in you we will ever trust,
    in you day by day we put our hope,
    for you are the God of love,
    today, tomorrow and for ever.
Amen.
(T. Sullivan-Vaughan, King's College)

6. *A world in harmony*

A NEW WORLD

God of Goodness and Truth,
    we have lots to do in your world.
The teaching of your Son, Jesus Christ, is like a measuring rod
    by which we can see what is straight and true.
Let his words sink into our hearts and minds
    so that we become sensitive
    to what is of value and what is worthless,
then give us the courage to stand up for truth and integrity,
    kindness and caring.

Help us to gain our self-esteem from your love,
    and then build up others to see themselves
    as your beloved sons and daughters,
    capable of bringing sanity to a confused world.

God, you hold the future in your purpose;
    by your Holy Spirit assist us to work for harmony,
    justice and wholeness among all people.
We make this prayer with Christ, our Saviour and our God.
Amen.

(Peter Atkins)

THE PLANET EARTH

God, Creator and Sustainer of life,
    help us to understand how precious our world is,
    to take care of its life and its resources,
    to be aware how fragile the environment is,
    and to be satisfied with what we have.
    Forgive our selfishness in destroying your Creation,
    and give us the wisdom and strength to look after the planet earth;
    for your love's sake.
Amen.

(Janis Cheng, Diocesan School)

LEADERS OF TOMORROW

Creator God, your plan for the universe
    was born out of generosity, order and purpose.
Yet humanity has often spoilt your plan
    by self-centred greed, and jealousy

of the achievements of others.
Forgive us and restore us.
Enabling God, you call men and women
to be the leaders of your people,
and bestow on them your Holy Spirit
to empower them for their work.
Help a new generation to train for their responsibilities
as the leaders of tomorrow.
Give them vision and insight, boldness and humility.
Make them able to sift the good from the bad,
the true from the false, the loving from the hating.
Give them a keen eye to discern the differences,
and firm feet to follow your way;
ever committed to the teaching and example
of your Son, Jesus Christ;
in whose name we make this prayer.
Amen.
(Peter Atkins)

LEADERS FOR THE NEW GENERATION
God of Guidance,
give us leaders for the future who will be thinking of others,
not only of themselves,
who have a sense of humour,
who stand up for what they think is right,
no matter if everyone disagrees with them.
Help them to be kind, cooperative and organized,
and help us all to encourage our leaders,
and to look up to them,
as we do to your Son Jesus Christ our Lord.
Amen.
(Qiulae Wong, Diocesan School)

SHALOM
Dear Lord,
you have created us in your own image
to take care of each other;
yet as the millennium approaches we are under great stress,
and many are drifting away from you.
We too find ourselves under peer pressure,

and you are relegated to the back of our minds
as we fill the world with evil.
Show us that we *can* love each other,
and *can* act as a whole body together,
so that we can all have a place in your purpose
and at last know your peace,
through Jesus Christ our Saviour.
Amen.
(Nicholas Moss, King's College)

A PRAYER FOR PEACE
Prince of Peace,
by your Holy Spirit,
give –
peace in our hearts;
peace in our families;
peace amidst the stress of today's workplace;
peace and contentment to those who've found
that money will not satisfy;
peace between the different races in our land;
peace between the nations;
and in the silence of your peace
may we hear again your blessing:
'Peace be with you.
My peace I give to you.'
Alleluia. Amen.
(Rosemary Atkins)

A NEW WORLD
Dear God,
may we draw on your strength and guidance
so that we can appreciate this world you have given to us;
may racial boundaries crumple in our hearts
and the words of Christ beckon us to be a better people;
may you keep your wisdom open to us in time of need,
and answer our whims with thought-provoking silence,
so that we can stand up and carry your banner with conviction
along the endless road of time;
may you refresh the thirst of goodness
when we fall, struck with disillusionment.

Above all,
   help us to think of others like ourselves, not different or inferior,
   but casting the same colour in your eye, and in ours.
Please God,
   make your strength available to us to harness,
   then Heaven can be on Earth, if we fulfil the trust you gave us
   since the moment when you breathed life into the dormant world,
   your new world – and ours too.
Amen.
(Ben Ford, King's College)

7. *Partners in prayer and work*

A YOUNG PERSON'S PRAYER

Lord, my God,
I thank you that every single person is special to you
   and that you care about what happens to them.
I pray especially for those kids who think that they need
   drugs and alcohol to make them feel good about themselves.
Guide them to find a better way to enjoy life,
   and help them remember that they matter to you.
   Get the message through to them that in you they will find peace
   and a purpose and meaning for their lives.
Lord God,
   I pray also for our world community.
   Help rich and poor people of different communities
   to live as friends without prejudice or friction.
   Make people realize that it is what a person's heart is like inside
   that counts – not colour, race, where you live,
   or the label on your clothes.
I know the real heroes of today are those that find time in their lives
   to notice the needs of those around them,
   to lend a helping hand, and to be a friend.
   Out of my day-to-day friendship with you, my Lord,
   make me a hero too.
Amen.
(I. Sullivan, King's College)

A PRAYER FOR FORGIVENESS

Dear Lord, our God,
   please forgive us,

138

accept that we are not perfect,
    and forgive us for every sin:
  for every mean thing we do or say,
  for every selfish time we ignore you and turn away,
  for every occasion we forget what you have done for us,
please forgive us.
As our world progresses on and on into the future,
  we will make many more sins,
  stand by us because we love you, dear God
  even if some do not show it;
  and please go on forgiving us.
Dear God, assist and guide us not to make so many sins,
  but instead learn to treat you and each other
  with the respect that we should;
  for yours is the kingdom, the power and the glory,
  now, and in the future,
  2000 AD and onwards,
  even for ever and ever.
Amen.
(W. Brown, King's College)

A RESPONSIVE PRAYER FOR GUIDANCE

Guide us, O Lord, as we face the issues of the future:
Help us all to make the right choices.
Guide us, O Lord, to learn and to grow from past experience:
Teach us wisdom for our future.
Guide us, O Lord, to care for the earth, your beautiful Creation:
Help us to love the world we live in.
Guide us, O Lord, as we head into the new millennium:
Lord, give us your guidance evermore.
Amen.
(Helen Cocker, Petra Carey and Elizabeth Davies,
Diocesan School)

INTO THE NEW MILLENNIUM

Holy Spirit of God,
  guide us into the future with care,
  and take us into the new millennium with love.
Caring God,
  love us until the day we die,

and we will love you on this earth,
and when we are with you for ever in heaven.
Amen.

(Melanie Luen, Diocesan School)

A PRAYER OF BLESSING FOR THE FUTURE

May God, our Leader, guide each pilgrim step you take
on your journey:
may God's vision remain clear before you;
may God's presence be a strong support beneath you;
may God's perseverance be your continuing initiative,
and God's joy the warmth of the heart within you.
May Christ, our Companion, sharing life and love with his friends,
renew your commitment to serve him,
and empower your ministry –
however and wherever it may unfold.
May the Spirit, our Sustainer, enhance your talents
and deepen your faith,
and give to others the humility
to receive and use your gifts with joy.
May God, the Holy Trinity, continue to bless you,
so that you may be a blessing to all you meet
on your journey,
this day, and the next day,
and all the days of your life.
Amen.

(Peter Atkins)

An intercession of thanksgiving and hope for a new millennium

During this Intercession it is suggested that a series of candles be lit as the offerings of prayer are made. One large candle symbolizes Christ as Light to the World, and smaller candles stand for each topic of intercession. The Leader stands by the candles and is assisted in the lighting of the candles by members of the congregation. In the prayers the people respond with the words in bold type.

The Leader invites the people to join in the sequence of Intercession, saying:

Let us offer our prayers of thanksgiving and seek forgiveness
from the God of mercy and encouragement.

God of all the Ages, we thank you for your hand in Creation:
For the past in which you have guided us safely.
God of this Age, we thank you for the beginning of a new
    millennium:
**For this special time in history and for our place in this
    generation.**
God of everlasting mercy, at this time we ask you to forgive us:
for all the problems we create,
for all the harm we do,
for the poverty we make,
for the lifestyle and the living
which keep us and your world unhealthy.
God of mercy, forgive us and heal us.

After a pause the Leader says:

Jesus, Saviour of the World,
shine upon us with your forgiving love.

The large candle is lit.

Jesus, Light of the World,
We thank you that you cleanse and renew us.
We lift up our prayers to you,
joining in your intercessions for the world.

The first smaller candle is lit.

God of the heavens,
we thank you for the sun and moon and stars.
Keep a star alight for all young people:
May they prosper and grow,
taking up the challenges and opportunities for good.

The second smaller candle is lit.

God of the earth and sea, of mountains and trees,
shelter the peoples of the world from harm:

Protect us and guide us,
keep us from poverty and greed,
from war and hatred.

The third candle is lit.

God of desert and light, of fertile valley and night,
let the blessing of your sunshine and dew
fall on the communities of the world:
Help us to build security and respect
as the sound foundation for growing harmony and love.

The fourth candle is lit.

God of the new millennium, bless this generation with courage:
Help us to work out new solutions to our problems
and to excel in cooperation and goodwill towards one another.

The fifth candle is lit.

God of all time, all peoples and every creature,
renew the earth, protect your creatures,
and restore humanity with your wisdom:
Help us to share this planet responsibly,
and inspire us with vision for a better world.
Lord, our hopes and dreams we give with love to you.

The sixth candle is lit.

God of gentleness and compassion,
we pray for those hurt by sickness,
trouble, anxiety and catastrophe:
Cradle everyone gently in the palm of your hand,
support us and heal us in our times of need.

The seventh candle is lit.

God of the future,
continue to bring light and love to your Creation:
Banish the darkness in your world,
and let the new dawn refresh our pledge to serve you.

Lord, hear us:
Lord, hear our prayer.

In darkness and in light,
in trouble and in joy,
help us, gracious God,
to trust your purpose
and to praise your name,
through Jesus Christ our Saviour.
Amen.
(St Hilda's Collegiate School, Dunedin)

9

PRAYERS AND REFLECTIONS FOR PERSONAL WORSHIP

In this chapter I have gathered together some prayers and reflections which I offer to individuals to assist their worship at the beginning of a new millennium. There is a variety of styles and subjects to meet the different preferences that people have for their times of prayer and reflection. For those who wish to include reflection on passages of Scripture and on the wisdom of this generation, I encourage the use of the Scripture readings in Chapter 8 and of the words of wisdom in Chapter 10. I have begun the prayers in this chapter with a series of focused words under the title 'Brief prayers – deep thoughts', which in a few phrases encapsulate our feelings and relationships in prayer. There follow some prayers in the nature of 'Dialogue with God'. Finally there are some reflections on 'Life in the new millennium'. My hope is that these prayers and reflections will deepen the spirituality of my readers and provide them with 'leaping-points' in their relationship with God in prayer.

BRIEF PRAYERS – DEEP THOUGHTS

God

Omnipotent, Strong,
Watching over us,
We reverence your name;
Almighty.
(D. Lyall, King's College)

God

Our Father,
Ever loving us,
Good, powerful, only deity;
Love.
(T. Sullivan-Vaughan, King's College)

2000

New Millennium,
Dawning, hope, looming, anxiety,
World peace or chaos;
Technology.
(M. Rothwell, King's College)

Prayer

Heavenly conversations,
Talking, asking, rejoicing,
Reaching out to God;
Thanksgiving.
(A. Fraser, King's College)

Prayer

Understanding yourself,
Getting in touch,
Asking for God's forgiveness;
Contemplation.
(D. Henry, King's College)

Redemption

Forgiveness, Absolution,
Deliverance from sin,
Liberation;
Freedom!
(B. Ford, King's College)

Consolation

Comforting help,
God's unconditional support,
Encouragement, loyalty, friendship, love;
Solace.
(A. Chchima, King's College)

Peace

When the power of love
overpowers
the love of power,
the world will find
Peace.
(Donna MacGregor, Diocesan School)

Mutuality

Let patience and tolerance
be the fundamental tools
of our acceptance
of one another.
(Sarah Gatward, Diocesan School)

DIALOGUE WITH GOD

God, you are there

Dear God,
  I know that we sometimes forget about you,
  and we don't acknowledge the fact that you are there;
  but whenever we need you, you pay attention to us and listen
  for however long we need you.
  Even when we forget, and we seem to be doing fine,
  you are still always there,
  looking out for us, keeping us safe,
  being everything we need.
For being like that, I want to say, dear God,

thank you,
always.
(A pupil of King's College)

You are everything to me

God,
    when I ask for your forgiveness –   you forgive me;
    when I ask for your love –   you embrace me;
    when I ask for a friend –   you are there;
    when I need a ray of sunshine –   you send it;
    when I can't walk any further –   you carry me;
    when I am starving –   you feed me;
    when I am in despair –   you give me hope;
    when I am confused –   you give me wisdom;
    when you love me –   I learn to love you back.
(Clare Morton, Diocesan School)

The mist

Creator God,
    Bless the wings of the wood-pigeon
    that flies over the shadowless trees.
    Cast your light on the sprawling mountainsides,
    and on the crystal-blue sea that sparkles in your glory.
    Cleanse our souls like the weeping rivers and streams,
    and breathe life into our hearts,
    as you would blow the gentle sea winds.
    Clear away the mist from our eyes,
    so that we, like the environment around us,
    might live to praise your name.
(Julia Hanna, Diocesan School)

My guardian angel

Angel of God,
my guardian dear,
to God's true love,
admit me here.
    Ever this night,

ever this day,
be at my side,
to light up my way.
Guard and defend me,
guide my slow step,
my rule in life be,
my hope protect.
   Angel of God,
   my guardian dear,
   draw near and listen,
   to this my prayer.
(C. Stevenson, King's College)

Looking and finding

Caring God,
   I look for you at every moment;
   when I walk on the street
   and smile to you just passing by;
   when I play on the court
   and toss the ball for you to catch;
   when I fall to the ground
   and you give me your hand to help me up.
      Sometimes it is hard
      to keep looking for you, my God;
      when I can't find you there
      I feel I am sinking into a deep swamp.
   But you always come back to me
   when I lose you.
   Maybe it is me who doesn't realize
   that you are the one who looks for me.
      So please, my Father God, find me,
      and let me find you.
(Rak Hee Hwang, Diocesan School)

LIFE IN THE NEW MILLENNIUM

The other side of the fence

The grass is not in fact always greener
on the other side of the fence.
No, not at all.
Fences have nothing to do with it.
The grass is greenest wherever it is watered.
When crossing over fences, carry the water with you,
and tend to the grass,
wherever you may be.
(R. Johnston, King's College)

Our religion

Christ rejected,
kicked like a decayed football,
elbows skinned, knees shredded –
no longer able to stand tall –
a mesh of ribs – God beheaded.

Then, resurrection –
his body draped in white,
and his head glittering like tinsel,
with broken handcuffs of chrome.

A boy kneels before him and said:
'My knees hurt, I want to go back home.'
A woman stands, book in hand and sings,
as carefully as she says a prayer.
Bride and groom come to exchange the rings,
proudly saying 'I do' for all to hear.

Even though constantly rejected,
God will come and reward the neglected.
(J. Wong, King's College)

Hopes for a new millennium

A new millennium approaches
bringing fear, uncertainty, yet hope.

Let the people have courage to
      face their uncertainty,
      challenge their fears,
      and use their hope.
And more important still,
let the people learn:
      learn from past mistakes and injustices;
      learn that it is OK to be wrong if from it you learn to do
         right;
      learn to communicate with others;
and –   learn to understand those with fear, uncertainty, and hope.
(G. Deverell, King's College)

May wishes come true

Loving God,
I wish for a world
   where there is no war,
   where there is no hunger,
   where there is no prejudice,
   where there is no pollution.
O my God,
I wish for a world,
   where all the animals run free,
   where everyone has enough,
   where everyone could be friends,
   where everyone is happy,
in and through your love.
(Amy Wilkinson and Kate Walker,
Diocesan School)

Personal goals for the new millennium

- To use our environment with care.
- To stop all violence, in homes, on the streets, between countries, and everywhere else.
- To promote peace with all my fellow human beings.
- To make at least one contribution to help the entire world.
- To do my best to achieve greatness in whatever career I wish to pursue.

- To take responsibility for my own future, and not to have it decided for me.
- Never to get stuck in a rut, to try to make every day different, every day count.
- To help everyone have an even chance in life.
- To have fun in whatever I am doing.
- To call on God to help me achieve my goals.

(W. Ormiston, M. Rothwell and G. Rhodes,
King's College)

Community aims for a new century

- To take away the nuclear threat.
- To eliminate racial prejudice.
- To cut automobile accidents due to speed and drink.
- To develop a cure for AIDS.
- To find a cure for cancer.
- To ban hunting, especially of endangered animals.
- To develop a mass-produced hybrid car.
- To stop polluting the environment.
- To gain world peace.
- To stop famine.

What is my role in helping the community to achieve these aims?
(S. Weatherston, G. Williams, S. Abbott and G. Panther,
King's College)

The millennium man

A silent man walks down the street,
with tears trickling from his eyes,
looking at the homeless and poor,
seeking shelter from the darkening skies.

He stops at every single one,
leaving food or money or clothes,
himself walking barefoot and ragged,
while he sees the rich who have so much to own.

As to who this mysterious man may be,
is neither the question nor a clue,

he follows God's word and does what's right,
and who he is, you can choose.
(William Eivers, King's College)

Children

Today, children are the future;
Tomorrow, our leaders.
The earth is the stage of their lives;
Respect for them both
Will result in a brighter
Millennium.
(Katie MacKinlay and Claire Wheeler,
Diocesan School)

Mother earth

God, Creator of our world,
    we thank you for the clear blue sky,
    for the green, green grass.
We too are sad,
    when people spoil your world,
    by pollution and burning,
    by wars and violence,
    by abuse to people and cruelty to animals.
Help us to make a difference
    so that every creature is free
    and every person is happy;
    that mother earth is healthy
    and is our friend.
(St Hilda's Collegiate School*)

Our world

God,
    you care for everything in this world,
    but we have not taken care
    of what you have given us.
    There are poor people,
    and there are people who have too much.

There are people who are thankful for what they have,
and there are people who are not.
That's how war starts.
Please God,
help me to be thankful for what I have,
and not to want more than I need,
so that together our world can live in peace.
(St Hilda's Collegiate School*)

In a world of millions

When I go to sleep at night
across the globe others fight.
I wish they'd stop and see
what hurts others, hurts me –
one small child,
in a world of millions.
Power produces cruel fate;
greed is dangerous, so is hate;
To leaders thinking they have a right
to take up arms and start a fight –
this point I make to them, and say,
that, though I'm only one,
in a world of millions,
so are they!
(St Hilda's Collegiate School*)

Our leaders

Lord God, Father of this universe,
you made everything for good,
but sometimes I am afraid
that not everything is as you intended.
In the new millennium,
help our leaders to work together,
to make a difference;
then people will have a place to warm their hands,
children will have homes and schools,
animals will live in safety,
everyone will have an equal share of money and health,

guns will be restrained,
>and the world and its peoples will live in peace,
as you intended.
(St Hilda's Collegiate School*)

*Contributors from St Hilda's Collegiate School, Dunedin were: Polly Higbee, Anna Kelly, Michalle Hagan, Rachael Elder, Anna Garland, Kylie Matheson, and the School's Chaplain, the Reverend Erice Fairbrother.

10

MESSAGES FOR A NEW MILLENNIUM

I have collected together a series of messages written by some representative Church leaders and Christian scholars from throughout the world, who bring to us their wisdom and vision on significant themes for the year 2000. These are suitable passages for reading to a congregation as part of special occasions of worship during the opening years of the third millennium, and for private meditation in our personal devotions during this time. Many of these contributions have been written especially for this book, while others are extracts from larger works produced for the new millennium. The name of the contributor is attached to each passage, and a full list of the contributors is found in Chapter 6. I have given a title to each passage which can be announced before the reading to focus our minds on the topic. It is important that we listen closely to these messages, as they come from the prophets of today and concern the issues that will face us as the new millennium begins.

FROM GLOBAL LEADERS

The Pope

Celebrating a Great Jubilee year
From the beginning of my pontificate I have had the opportunity to speak explicitly of the Great Jubilee, inviting all to live the period of expectation as 'a new advent'. The Jubilee of the year 2000 is meant to be a great prayer

of praise and thanksgiving especially for the gift of the Incarnation of the Son of God and of the Redemption which he accomplished.

The Spirit's message

In this period it is necessary to increase our sensitivity to 'what the Spirit is suggesting' to the different communities, from the smallest ones, such as the family, to the largest ones, such as nations and international organizations, taking into account cultures, societies and sound traditions. Despite appearances humanity continues to await the revelation of the children of God, and lives by this hope like a mother in labour, to use the image employed so powerfully by St Paul in his Letter to the Romans (8:19–22).

Hope

The Great Jubilee will enable humanity to cross the threshold of the third millennium as a threshold of genuine hope. The basic attitude of hope, on the one hand, encourages the Christians not to lose sight of the final goal which gives meaning and value to life, and on the other, offers solid and profound reasons for a daily commitment to transform reality in order to make it correspond to God's plan.

Unity

The approaching end of the second millennium demands of everyone an examination of conscience and the promotion of fitting ecumenical initiatives, so that we can celebrate the Great Jubilee, if not completely united, at least much closer to overcoming the divisions of the second millennium.

Faith

Dear brothers and sisters, let us pray that this event will be fulfilled, according to God's will, as a moment of an intense deepening of faith. The Jubilee celebration should confirm the Christians of today in their faith in God who has revealed himself in Christ, sustain their hope which reaches out in expectation of eternal life, and rekindle their charity in active service to their brothers and sisters. Acknowledging the weaknesses of the past is an act of honesty and courage which helps us to strengthen our faith, which alerts us to face today's temptations and challenges, and prepares us to meet them.

Family

Each family, in some way, should be involved in the preparations for the Great Jubilee. Was it not through a family, the family of Nazareth, that the Son of God chose to enter into human history?

The future
The future of the world and of the Church belongs to the younger generation, to those who, born in this century, will reach maturity in the next, the
first century of the new millennium. Christ expects great things from
young people, as he did from the young man who asked him:'What good
deed must I do to have eternal life?'(Matthew 19:16)

Social justice
A commitment to justice and peace in a world like ours, marked by so
many conflicts and intolerable social and economic inequalities, is a
necessary condition for the preparation and celebration of the Jubilee.
Christians will have to raise their voices [about] … the international debt
… the differences of dialogue between different cultures … respect for
women's rights, and the promotion of family and marriage.

The mass media
Today everyone is aware of how important it is not to neglect the world of
communications,'the first areopagus of modern times', uniting humanity
which has become, as is often said,'a global village'. Such a commitment
does not only aim at extending the proclamation; it is concerned with
something deeper, since the very evangelization of modern culture
depends to a large extent on the influence of the mass media.

(John Paul II,Vatican, Rome)

(The above extracts were taken from his Apostolic Letter,'On the Coming
of the Third Millennium' (*'Tertio Millennio adveniente'*) (10 November
1994), and from his Address to the Central Committee of the Great Jubilee
of theYear 2000.)

The Archbishop of Canterbury

A common commitment to service
One of the greatest privileges I have had since becoming Archbishop of
Canterbury in 1991 is to have seen something of the Mission and Ministry
of the Churches around the world. They differ in many ways but what
binds them together is a common commitment to serving Christ and their
fellow human beings in the societies and cultures to which they belong.

The Christian ethic in practice

The ethic of 'loving one's neighbour as oneself' is something that should inform our thinking at every level, and one of my joys has been to discover that it often does so in practice – whether in teaching the young; campaigning for social justice; caring for the sick and suffering; feeding the hungry; or showing Christ's compassion in any one of a thousand ways.

The Church's credibility in a new millennium

As the New Millennium dawns I remain convinced that the most effective way of proclaiming the Gospel is to live it out in our lives, and then to speak of Christ in that context. Here in England we set up the Church Urban Fund in 1988 to sponsor a wide variety of projects in our Inner Cities. I remember the response of one of the clergy to a question about its impact on his community. His reply was very simple: 'It has made the Church credible', and that is something I long to see echoed time and again, all around the world, as the new Millennium unfolds.

(George Cantuar, Lambeth Palace, London)

The General Secretary of the World Council of Churches

Joy and unity

Celebrating an anniversary is an activity that takes place in a time and space which are set apart. Food and drink are saved for the occasion. In celebration, human beings are able to transcend the scarcities and limitations of everyday life. Joy is the emotion which expresses the experience of overflowing abundance and gratuity of life.

The future

Perceptive observers agree that the present course of human development cannot be sustained in the long run. Even without indulging in apocalyptic prophecies, we can recognize clearly that the meeting of the challenges of the new century will require a fundamental reorientation in the forms of human life. The changes required go beyond scientific, technological or structural innovations and reach into the spiritual and moral foundations of humanity.

Life-centredness requires us to learn a relationship of caring for all living beings and for all processes which sustain human life. Human needs will have to be brought into a new balance with the needs and capabilities for regenerating life through the life-cycles. Human history will have to be reassessed as an important but limited part of the history of nature.

Unity

There is hope that the possibilities offered to the churches by the year 2000 for a genuinely common witness and for a renewed commitment to the unity of the Church can be realized. Such a commemoration will be a witness to Jesus Christ as the source of faith, hope and love only if it addresses the hopes and fears, expectations and anxieties among people today in view of the changes affecting their lives as the third millennium approaches. Important as it is to remember the way of the Church during the outgoing millennium in a spirit of repentance and joyful celebration, what is essential will be engaging together in discerning the signs of the time, so that the commemoration of the year 2000 might become an invitation to a renewal in the life and witness of the Church.

(Dr Konrad Raiser, Geneva)

(The above extracts were taken from *To be the Church – Challenges and Hopes for a New Millennium* [WCC Publications, Geneva, 1997].)

The World Wide President of the Mothers' Union

Families in the new millennium

Thoughts of the millennium are exciting, dramatic, confusing, invigorating, and for Christian people also very challenging. For we who profess to follow Christ have much to ponder at this time:

First how to proclaim effectively that this new dawn is a celebration of Christ's life, and refuse to allow the secular world to claim it for itself.

Secondly we must hold the balance between maintaining the traditions of the past, and engaging in the promises of the future.

In the closing years of the twentieth century the family as the accepted basic building-block of society has come under increasing attack, often subtle but nonetheless erosive. Yet as I have travelled the world on behalf of the Mothers' Union I have seen family life experienced in many diverse situations: refugee camps where pilgrim people seek transient shelter; displaced-persons' camps in places where man's inhumanity to man has caused unimaginable suffering; against a backdrop of wealth and poverty. Repeatedly I have marvelled at the Christian witness of so many, and the certainty and knowledge of God's love which has sustained them in such situations.

The new millennium is an opportunity for us to restate the centrality of the family: that it is the best basic building-block of society, and that our global community diminishes it at its peril. Rather we should redouble our efforts to make family life in all its diversity, both of interpretation and situation, the best it can be. It is then for the Christian community to state and to practise that it is in a *family* that the Christ-taught qualities of love, tolerance, justice, discipline and respect for each unique individual made in the image of God, are best absorbed, so that each person may be enabled to reach out to the promise of the future.

(Lady Christine Eames, Mary Sumner House, London)

A message from young people

A moral code for the new millennium
- To help those suffering from poverty and hunger.
- To raise spiritual awareness.
- To decrease materialism in society by focusing on moral values.
- To develop better tolerance for others whatever their gender, race or creed.
- To understand more fully the problems of our fellow human beings.
- To solve conflicts peacefully, without resorting to war and violence.
- To focus on the family as the heart of society.
- To render help whenever and wherever we can.
- To make health a top priority as a basic human need, instead of seeing it as a business.
- To further the freedom of speech and justice.

(Pupils at King's College, Auckland, New Zealand)

FROM THE REGIONS OF THE WORLD

The President of the China Christian Council

Outreach and joy
Each time we talk about the year 2000, we actually affirm once more the glory of that lowly carpenter of Nazareth. Time is counted by his birth and earthly life. In doing so humankind recognizes him to be the centre of history.

Jesus Christ is the one central subject of Christian witness and of Christian adoration. Life becomes so much the poorer without his incarnation. I am an age-witness not only to the influx of new disciples in response to the Church's evangelistic outreach in almost every part of

China, but also to the joy and felicity on the part of an increasing number of my compatriots who find in Christian worship their enrichment and fulfilment.

The year 2000 will usher in a new period of growth in numbers as well as in spirituality in China and elsewhere. This is my earnest prayer.

(Han Wenzao, Nanjing, China)

The Bishop of Johannesburg

A vision of transformation

We dream such a wonderful dream in our land. We have lived through the nightmare; we have seen the reality of the nightmare emerge as we have heard, through the Truth and Reconciliation Commission, what happened – systematically, cold-bloodedly and with no mercy. We have seen the response – violence and cruelty begets violence – but above all we have seen a desire to face the truth and forgive; to look at our corporate ugliness, our spurious strength and our accepted weakness, and live as people who *need* to live together in peace and justice.

We are also seeing the results of transition: violence, crime, insecurity, corruption, rape, fear, *and* amazing goodness. We live with all of this, and we are still the people of South Africa, struggling to a new vision of transformation. We dream of goodness and a life of peace for all; of courage and work, satisfying and creative work for all; of laughter and the joy of seeing the best in each other; and of justice widespread and corruption rooted out.

For those who have eyes to see, all good things come as we try to be obedient to the one who washes our feet, who dies for us and lives for us, who calls us to forgive and judge not, so that the one who judges justly may see the true nature of who we are and why we believe as we do. Above all we will find him when, humble and penitent, joyful and bursting with his risen life, we kneel and receive him at the altar, the table of God's people, as he gives himself to sustain us for the vision and the journey.

(Duncan Buchanan, Johannesburg, South Africa)

The Executive Director of the Association for Theological Education in South East Asia

Peace-makers and justice-doers

The significance of the year 2000 for Christians is just too obvious for all who identify themselves as peace-makers and justice-doers, so much so that we ignore it at our peril. There is still need to enter into, participate in, and gather up the pains of the suffering millions of women, men and children in Asia. There is still so much pain in our gain.

So I invite you to join in and swell the number of that small band of brave and committed Christians who are dedicated to the full liberation of all the world. No one is free unless everyone is free. To be with the oppressed women in Asia and the oppressed in the world is to be in solidarity with the people who hold up half the sky. Silently, but surely, Jesus has been the rallying point for numerous Asian women to straighten themselves. They have learnt that they do not need to be bent over. They don't need to suffer from the spirit of infirmity.

Touch a hand.
Make a friend.

(The Revd Dr Yeow Choo-Lak, Manila, Philippines)

(The above extract is taken from 'Bent over no more – a Meditation on Luke 13:10–17'.)

The Anglican Bishop of Polynesia and Secretary of the South Pacific Anglican Council

The voice of the Pacific

The Christian Faith was introduced to these islands less than 200 years ago, and in some quarters it still needs to be rooted in depth in the life of our people. Most Pacific islands have changed their way of life in the light of the coming of the Gospel. The dignity of human life, the value of family life, the sharing and caring for one's neighbour are some of the Christian teachings that have prevailed. However, there are in some quarters undercurrents of inherent cultural practices and values that sometimes seem to be in conflict with the Christian Faith.

Pacific Island Christians will celebrate the year 2000 as a significant event because of their Christian faith. They recognize this year as the 'Year of our Lord'. Strategically positioned with the International

Date-line, they will be the first region in the world to welcome the new millennium.

(Jabez Bryce, Suva, Fiji)

The Bishop of Dunedin in the Anglican Church in Aotearoa, New Zealand and Polynesia

Time and light on southern shores

The Diocese of Dunedin is the most southern in the world. We will be among the first to greet the new millennium in the early hours of a summer morning. Our mountains will welcome it, and our people, relaxing during our holiday time, will mark it gently as the passing of a significant time-mark. It is a peaceful time of year, and time itself is founded on the timely arrival of the Prince of Peace, Christ our Lord.

As we delight anew in the wonderful gifts of creation that we have received from God in this southern part of God's vineyard, with its mountains, lakes, sea-shore, forests, and high country plains, we will watch the sunlight roll on across continents, islands and oceans, turning darkness to light, and opening up a span of time that will last beyond the span of any mortal being.

Time and eternity converge at that still point of the turning world; and truly the timelessness of our God, who chose us to live in time and make mortality sacred, is sharpened like light through glass.

May we burn with the love of God, who loves us more intensely than we can possibly imagine.

(Penny Jamieson, Dunedin, New Zealand)

The Bishop of Newcastle, Australia and Chaplain at the 1998 Lambeth Conference

Australians go for gold

For Australians, and to those of us living under the shadow of the City of Sydney, the year 2000 marks the Olympics and the Paralympics. Our attention and energy seem to focus on nothing else. Whilst in the UK the construction of the Millennium Dome has brought controversy surrounding what should be represented in it – given that Britain sees itself as a multi-faith society – in Australia the religion of sport and our desire to win more gold overshadows other factors of the millennium.

We are a quasi-religious society. This was well described by a journalist who outlined the embarrassment at the millionaire jockey Darren Beadman's conversion to Christianity:

> Unlike the zealous Pilgrims who stumbled into America's shores seeking freedom of religious expression, Australia's convict ancestors would have preferred a good drink and a gamble, and we still do. Hence our Beadman dilemma: a millionaire jockey (riding a horse named Saintly!) gives up a life that thousands of Australians would kill for, and turns to the God we turned away from long ago. It stuns us; it positively embarrasses us. Saintly's trainer, Bart Cummings, managed to suggest that Beadman may need a second opinion. In a country where religious apathy is our version of religious tolerance, that's as close to religious persecution as an Australian can get.

It is easy to see why we in Australia have a 'millennium black-out'!

A celebration of faith
As a young boy growing up in Sri Lanka I remember very vividly how that community celebrated the Buddha Jayanthi – 2500 years since the birth, emancipation, death and entry into the state of Nirvana of Siddhartha Gauthama – the Buddha. The faith element marked every aspect of the year of festivity. Processions, concerts, street fairs, newly minted coins, special issue stamps, every national event was linked in no unmistakable way to the Buddhist faith.

The millennium should mark, to all intents and purposes, the birth, death, resurrection of Jesus of Nazareth. Yet, because the 'BC/AD' factor belongs to the world there is a tendency, particularly in nations with a liberal democratic heritage, to play down the foundation of the millennium. This sensitivity is seen in the decision made by modern writers of history to describe the years before and after the Christ event in terms of 'BCE' and 'CE'. Our rational mind, so bound in the relativization of Truth, blushes when it comes to highlighting that which stands at the centre of our civilization, its history and that which forms our psyche.

Core values for the new millennium
In the name of multi-culturalism we cover up that which is formative of our core values – God loved us so deeply that at a point of time in our history, God entered the dust of our lives so fully that in that human being, Jesus, we glimpsed what the dignity of life and humanness is all about. The

Cross and Resurrection are ways of informing, inspiring, intimating to us that we are created not to wilt at our failure, weakness and shortcomings, but to remind ourselves how precious we are to God. This truth expresses itself in our every relationship – be it at home, school, community, the work-place, the whole created order, and calls us to treat all aspects of living and dying with profound love and reverence. Repentance, the turning around from the old to the new, is because Love makes the radical change possible.

For me the underplaying of the Christian Faith element in the celebrations of the millennium has an irony attached to it. In loving the world so much God gave – a giving that ends in a snuffing out (the crucifixion). The resurrection is God's way of saying that love, though it may be ignored, side-lined, crushed, still wins out. Perhaps as a Christian community we may need to discover again that kind of love, which gives itself so readily, desiring no gain and little recognition. Maybe then, the Truth of what took place 2000 years ago will be revealed to our world in a fresh way.

> Come Lord Jesus, in your total self-giving,
> that in that power
> our lives and the face of the earth
> may be renewed.

(Roger Herft, Newcastle, New South Wales)

The Bishop of Rochester, England and former Bishop in the United Church of Pakistan

A new start then, and now

The year 2000 has significance for me because it heralds the time from which the Gospel began to change the hearts and minds of men and women and, therefore, to change the structures of human society. The effects of this in terms of human freedom, equality and dignity have been far-reaching indeed, and they continue to reverberate down the ages.

Christians have not always been faithful in bringing the Gospel to bear on the needs of the world. The millennium gives us an opportunity for *a new start*:

- a new start in renewing our commitment to Christ;
- a new start in meeting the needs of our fellow human beings with the transformative power of the Gospel;

• and a new start in promoting justice and compassion in the world.

(The Rt Revd Dr Michael Nazir-Ali)

The Chairman of the Central Committee
of the Conference of European Churches

A challenge to the European churches

Every five hundred years or so, Europe goes through a great and complex convulsion, when an inherited pattern breaks up and a new one emerges. The first century of our era, which saw the establishment both of the Roman Empire and also of the Christian Church, was one such moment. The fall of the Roman Empire in the West, the end of the ancient world and the beginning of the Middle Ages in the fifth and sixth centuries was another. The schism between East and West, the end of the Viking era and the rise of the Papal Monarchy at the end of the first millennium formed yet another such complex, and the fall of Byzantium, the great discoveries, the Renaissance and the Reformation formed another.

Now once more the pattern of nation states in Europe and the pattern of church life developed at the time of the Reformation and the Counter-Reformation are both breaking up. So are the patterns of thought which went with them. People are confused by change; and, if they feel over-whelmed by change which they cannot understand, they fall back into the few certainties they think they do understand. Unfortunately, the only one which is widespread now is the kind of narrow nationalism which led to the disasters and catastrophes of two world wars in our century. At each of the four previous crises, Christian thinkers emerged to help people to interpret what was happening, not passively as fate but actively as part of God's providence. St Paul and the other New Testament writers in the first century, the Greek and Latin Fathers in the patristic period, these all did their work of interpretation in a unifying way. By contrast, the crises of a thousand years ago and five hundred years ago led to the fragmentation of the Church.

It is a challenge to the European churches, which have been the victims and the perpetrators of so much disunity, to work together now to accompany the peoples and nations of Europe into the next millennium with a message of peace, hope and unity.

(John Arnold, Dean, Durham, England)
(The extracts above are taken from the Chairman's Report to the XIth Assembly in Graz.)

SCHOLARS

The Professor of History, Ecole Biblique et Archéologique Française, Jerusalem

Christianity – rooted in the history of a people and the soil of a land

Christianity is more than an idea or an ideal. It is rooted in the history of a people and of a land. It is identified with a particular human individual, Jesus Christ, who was conceived at Nazareth and born at Bethlehem, who lived in Galilee and walked the roads of Samaria, Transjordan and Judea, and who died and rose again in Jerusalem. Those of us who have the privilege of living, even as foreigners, in this land, or who have had the opportunity of visiting it, know that our way of understanding the Faith has been profoundly changed by the experience. The Gospel story becomes concrete and vivid on the shores of the Sea of Galilee or in the crowded, narrow streets of Jerusalem.

Even the troubled politics of this land throw light on the Bible. Read the Old Testament or the New, and you will find not peace and concord, but hostility and division, and that is the way, it seems, it has always been. The Prince of Peace was born at a time and in a place of conflict. That is part of the reason why His person and His message are still relevant, 2000 years later.

(Justin Taylor SM, Jerusalem)

The Pro-Vice-Chancellor and Professor of Theology at the University of Birmingham, England

Significant moments of time

Anno Domini 2000 is an opportunity to reflect on the nature of time. For the artificiality of the date alerts us to the fact that time is largely a human construct, measured according to the conventions of cultures. Yet both 'time travel' and the 'reversal of the clock' seem fantastic notions, and we feel we live in a time-bound universe. So we devise ways of marking the passage of time chronologically, while knowing that in experience time goes fast or slow, and some moments or occasions are far more significant than others, both in history and in individual lives.

Significant moments shape our understanding of life, giving meaning to the otherwise meaningless succession of events measured in hours, weeks or years. And we can choose to relive such moments, structuring time as remembrance, as renewal of meaning. That is what happens in liturgy – the re-enactment of the significant moments when the eternal and sacred impinge upon time and the secular.

Maybe the year 2000, by being at once artificial and theoretically connected with the Incarnation, can be both a secular and Christian moment when people for once devise liturgies of recollection. Our self-conscious post-modern culture perhaps needs a reminder that

All people are grass...
The grass withers, the flower fades;
But the word of our God will stand forever. (From Isaiah 40:6–8)

(Frances Young, Birmingham, UK)

The Hugh Latimer Elderdice Professor of Preaching and Worship at Wesley Theological Seminary, Washington DC, USA

An opportunity to be a human family as God intended

Given the somewhat capricious way in which we have come to celebrate the years, we may wonder whether our millennium celebrations are of any interest to God at all. Perhaps the way humans calculate and observe new years and new centuries are of concern to us but not to the Almighty. The approach of each new year's day is perceived by us mortals as an opportunity for recapitulation, evaluation and reforma-tion. The close of each decade intensifies such an opportunity, and the end of every century presses the point even more urgently. But just ahead of us lies a distinctive opportunity. For we are the first people in history consciously to mark worldwide the close of one millennium and the advent of another, for in what we call the year 1000 many different calendrical systems prevailed. Even among those who shared our system, there were no means for information distribution and commu-nication to make possible a common observance. In this sense the coming of the year 2000 is truly unique.

Since God is our Maker, and since we reasonably ascribe to the Creator the essence of the creature, in the end the year 2000 may matter greatly to God after all – not because that number is metaphysically significant or onto-logically unique, but because to some degree the heart of the Maker must surely rejoice any time we creatures pause to reflect on the achievements and errors of the past in order that we may act more responsibly toward the chal-lenges of the future. And surely that same divine heart would rejoice immensely if for once all of humanity could pause (no matter how briefly) to contemplate together the purposes and goals of our common origin, nature, quest and destiny, and to consider the imperatives of justice and peace in our mutual existence. In such an endeavour we might indeed begin to be what God intends: a human family, not merely the human race.

Perhaps God is offering to the Christian community at this moment in history the opportunity to invite the adherents of every faith across the globe to join with us in just such an endeavour of assessment and amendment of life.

(Laurence Stookey, Washington DC, USA)

The Albert Cook Outler Professor of Wesley Studies, Perkins School of Theology, Dallas, USA

Learning from a saint of the past

We leave the second millennium and enter the third at a time when Christianity is at once exhausted and volatile. We have created a post-Christian world which has exposed our divisions as variations on a quest for chimerical foundations which are neither necessary nor healthy. We need the help of wise companions on the next leg of the journey.

I can think of no better mentor than the last great theologian of the Undivided Church, St Symeon the New Theologian, whose life spanned the end of the first and the birth of the second millennium from 949 to 1022. He was a charismatic Christian who believed passionately in the historic continuity of the Church; a priest who believed in the authority of laity as Christ-bearers to forgive sins; a Christian of deep assurance who had lasting sympathy for those yet seeking God; a person initiated into the riches of culture yet utterly captivated by the Gospel; a voice initially rejected but then pronounced truly faithful and canonical by the people of God; a theologian of extraordinary erudition who insisted that knowledge of God was beyond words; a figure who has twice been buried beneath the rubble of scholasticism but whose time has at last come in the history of the Church.

This St Symeon can become a true friend of us with God as we move into a new era. Whether we enter a new Dark Ages or encounter a Third Great Awakening, we will be deeply enriched by his wisdom, by his passion, and by the manifestation of the Spirit so powerfully present in his life and work.

(William J. Abraham, Dallas, USA)

The Chair of the Department of Moral and Practical Theology in the University of Auckland, New Zealand

Pastoral care in the new millennium

New social realities in those parts of the world with which I am familiar – the US, Europe, and the South Pacific – dictate that pastoral care in the coming millennium must be markedly different from its historical forms. Three factors in particular make it necessary for changes to be made in the manner and situation in which we carry out pastoral care.

The present model of pastoral care licenses lay and ordained ministers to a certain geographical location. Yet expanding electronic communications, unstable employment patterns, increased mobility, and the growing disconnection from traditional family structures, mean that people have less and less sense of loyalty to local parish structures. In the new millennium the call will be for ministry to go 'global' – moving beyond parochial boundaries to create new opportunities for ministry in unexpected places such as the Internet, a national pastoral care-call centre, or a city-wide specialist team, unbounded by geographical definitions.

In a democratic Church more and more laity are demanding opportunities to exercise ministries which are publicly honoured by the Church. Various forms of team ministry are emerging in which well-trained clergy are serving less as absolute authorities and more as facilitators *primus inter pares*, coordinating the ministry of a trained and responsible laity. The thrust of the future will be away from defining the ordained as pastoral experts and ritual specialists and towards seeing the ministry of all baptized Christians as agents of social care and change.

Governments in the regions I know are increasingly intruding into areas of teaching, care and healing which have traditionally been reserved to local church ministries. Yet with the rapid increase in population there are fewer resources to go around. Secular institutions and agencies are resorting to managed care policies, which severely curtail the amount and quality of the care and support available to those who need them most. In the face of this situation the Church of the new millennium is called, not to retreat, but to advance aggressively into new areas of care and support for the needy. The agents of the Church will seek to meet the hierarchy of the physical needs of people as well as their deep spiritual hunger.

The changes necessary to meet these challenges will require a dedicated and well-trained team of pastors – both lay and ordained – supported by the prayers and the gifts of the whole Church.

(Philip Culbertson, Auckland, New Zealand)

A younger generation of scholars

Ten goals for the new millennium

1. A complete worldwide ban on land-mines, chemical and biological weapons, and a cessation of further development of nuclear arsenals. The only possible reason for not having a total ban on nuclear weapons is that they can work as a powerful deterrent and prevent the cold wars from becoming full-blown conflicts. In the words of Kofi Annan, Secretary General of the United Nations: 'The true way of peace-keepers is to show force, so as never to need to use it.'

2. The settlement of major worldwide conflicts, especially those in Ireland, the Balkans and the Middle East that have boiled on for hundreds or even thousands of years, and are locked in such a perpetual stalemate that any settlement will require great strength, cooperation and perseverance.

3. A global community where people will become more accepting, and not discriminate against race, gender, colour or age, respecting others for who they are, not what they are. This will lead to a truly global community, and possibly in the next hundred years or so, to the merging of all countries into one, with a common purpose to help all humankind.

4. Cures for diseases that plague the human race, such as cancer, AIDS, ebola, and the common cold and 'flu. These cures need to be safe and available to people of every socio-economic status. This will lead to the improvement in the quality of life for millions of people and take away large amounts of sadness and suffering.

5. A new international language, with a phonetic alphabet, a simple structure, and derivations from all major languages. This would be taught in schools and understood by everyone. Again, this would be essential for all the world's countries to amalgamate into one.

6. A fuller consciousness about the environment, with emission levels cut to 0.1 per cent of the current standard. The human race will need to clean up the mess left behind by the destructive practices of the past. This is the only way that future billions will be able to enjoy our planet.

7. A new way of relating to others, putting the greed of our ancestors behind us, and instead giving help to those in need, working for reconciliation and better relationships. In this way we can be rewarded with the joy of giving and not the spite of taking. Those who have enough should not try to take things that they do not need and that poorer people might well require.

8. A better distribution of rewards where all receive money relative to the difficulty of their jobs, and not to the position they hold in an organization.

For example, a hard-working factory worker is entitled to more than a lazy managing director who sits around doing little.

9. Genetically engineered food that tastes good, and is very good for you. This would have to be cheap and readily available, especially in poorer countries. This would be an essential tool to curb shortages and eating disorders.

10. Good role models by public leaders, who need to set a good example and not destroy trust in them to the point that obvious lies about them can be easily believed. Young people also should be brought up as model citizens. This needs to start with families sticking together and not separating, which destroys a child mentally.

(Nicholas Moss, John Leightly, Lloyd Bahlmann and Shaun Sutton,
King's College, Auckland)

11

HYMNS AND
SONGS FOR A NEW
MILLENNIUM

In this small selection of words and music I have gathered together some examples of existing and new material, which I believe is suitable for use at celebrations of the year 2000 and the beginning of a new millennium.

The examples begin with two millennium hymns which were especially written at my invitation by Norman Brookes. The first echoes our note of thanksgiving to God with the title 'Give Thanks'; and the second, 'God of the Ages', reminds us that our God is the God of every time span, from the past to the future.

Then comes a group of three hymns which celebrate new beginnings with a vision of how Christians might act in a new world order. 'Here on the Threshold of a New Beginning' and 'Lord of the Years' are by the well-known English team of musical bishops, Timothy Dudley-Smith and Michael Baughen. The third, 'We Travel On', is my own composition to the Gaelic tune which we often use for the words 'Morning has broken'. I hope that this tune with the new words may give a chance for young people to sing this hymn, accompanied by recorders or the flute.

Seeing life as a journey, Colin Gibson has highlighted the God who walks beside us in his song 'It all depends'. I also asked Colin to compose a children's song to fit into the 'Service of the Spirit' in Chapter 7. He was inspired to write 'Kindness', a song for a two-part children's choir who would enjoy adding some actions. I am sure it will become popular with children and will also be used on more general occasions.

There follow three hymns with words by Shirley Murray. The first focuses on the guidance of God; the second on the Festival of Epiphany;

and the third reflects on the response of God to the actions of humanity. Jillian Bray provided the music for 'Where the Love of God is Guiding'. Colin Gibson's chromatic tune echoes the camel's hooves for the 'Song for Epiphany'. On reading Shirley Murray's references to God's compassion and longing in 'God Weeps', I was so touched that I responded with a new musical composition. There is therefore a choice of tunes between the one by Carlton R. Young, which is found in the collection *Every Day in Your Spirit*, and my own as arranged by Stanley Jackson, which I have called 'Compassion'.

I wanted to include some music in a modern idiom and sent a search request to a former student of mine now working in England. Jeremy Clark recommended the compositions of Matt Redman, and I am glad to include 'It's Rising Up', a joint work with Martin Smith, being number 835 from the *Songs of Fellowship Worship Resource, Music Book Two* (ISBN 0 85476 770 3). On the same page I indicate some other songs from the collection which are appropriate to our theme.

To complete this selection I needed a celebration song with a strong rhythm to encourage congregational singing. I am sure that we will find Michael Baughen's response to my search widely popular with those who wish to choose this style of singing. His title 'Come Celebrate' is my invitation to everyone to enter this new millennium with joyful songs and vibrant faith.

I refer readers to other collections which include hymns and songs for our celebrations. As I write I am aware of the Millennium Hymn Competition organized by Canon Michael Saward at St Paul's Cathedral in London, and of the collection *Singing in Celebration* by Jane Parker Huber (Westminster John Knox Press, Louisville, 1996). Collections of words and music by Colin Gibson and Shirley Murray have been published by Hope Publishing Company, and you will find the titles on the following pages.

All enquiries for permission to use these hymns and songs should be addressed to the copyright holders (whose addresses are shown after each hymn or song) or to their licence agent.

HYMNS AND
SONGS FOR A NEW
MILLENNIUM

1 Give thanks

THANKSGIVING 2000   86 86 86

Words: Norman E. Brookes
Music: Peter Atkins

Give thanks, give thanks for this new day, an of - fering from the Lord. A new mil - len - nium comes our way, it's ours to be ex - plored. May it with Chris - tian_ love be filled In it Christ's name a - dored.

1 Give thanks, give thanks for this new day,
 an offering from the Lord.
 A new millennium comes our way,
 it's ours to be explored.
 May it with Christian love be filled
 In it Christ's name adored.

2 Find faith, true faith for this new day,
 for challenge it will bring,
 that tests our faith, our truth, our way,
 our own best offering.
 With faith we can life's questions face,
 And Christ's light to them bring.

3 Find love, true love for this new day,
 it will God's love require.
 For human needs will come our way,
 and crises near and far.
 In these may Christ be seen afresh
 When we through love empower.

4 Find hope, sure hope for this new day,
 hope makes the three complete,
 for lives that demonstrate these marks
 all hatred can defeat.
 So let the word of Jesus speak
 As this new world we greet.

Requests for permission to reproduce the words should be addressed to the Revd N. Brookes, 12 Halberg Street, Papakura, Auckland, New Zealand (Tel/Fax: 0064–9–298 8110). Requests for permission to reproduce the music should be addressed to the author at 9A Paunui Street, Auckland 1005, New Zealand (Fax: 0064–9–5750477).

2

God of the ages

REPTON   86 88 66

Words: Norman E. Brookes
Music: C. H. H. Parry (1848–1918)

Great God, of a - ges___ back in time, e - -ter - nal with us now, the years we mea - sure by that sign Em - man - uel, born of your de - sign, a - -mong us long a - go, a - mong us long a - go.

1 Great God, of ages back in time,
  eternal with us now,
  the years we measure by that sign
  Emmanuel, born of your design,
  among us long ago,
  among us long ago.

2 Great God, of ages yet to be,
  beyond this day and hour,
  raise high the Christ who sets us free,
  inspire us by his love to be
  transforming signs of grace,
  transforming signs of grace.

3 Great God, of moments here and now,
  of time, of place, of race,
  transcend the walls that deep divide,
  let us in unity reside,
  and find in Christ a place,
  and find in Christ a place.

4 Now is the moment to affirm
  Christ's rule of life and time –
  two thousand years have come and gone,
  but still his vision calls us on
  to service in Christ's name,
  to service in Christ's name.

Requests for permission to reproduce the words should be addressed to the Revd N. Brookes, 12 Halberg Street, Papakura, Auckland, New Zealand (Tel/Fax: 0064–9–298 8110).

3   Here on the threshold of a new beginning

New Millennium   11 10 11 10 D

Words: Timothy Dudley-Smith
Music: Michael Baughen
arranged Gerard Brooks

Here on the thres-hold of a new be-gin-ning, by grace for-giv-en, now we leave be-hind our long-re-pent-ed self-ish-ness and sin-ning, and all our bles-sings call a-gain to mind: Christ to re-deem us, ran-som and re-store us, the love that holds us in a

Sa - viour's care, faith strong to wel-come all that lies be -

- fore us, our un-known fu - ture, know-ing God is there.

1 Here on the threshold of a new beginning,
  by grace forgiven, now we leave behind
  our long-repented selfishness and sinning,
  and all our blessings call again to mind:
  Christ to redeem us, ransom and restore us,
  the love that holds us in a Saviour's care,
  faith strong to welcome all that lies before us,
  our unknown future, knowing God is there.

2 May we, your children, feel with Christ's compassion
  an earth disordered, hungry and in pain;
  then, at your calling, find the will to fashion
  new ways where freedom, truth and justice reign;
  where wars are ended, ancient wrongs are righted,
  and nations value human life and worth;
  where in the darkness lamps of hope are lighted
  and Christ is honoured over all the earth.

3 So may your wisdom shine from Scripture's pages
  to mould and make us stones with which to build
  God's holy temple, through eternal ages,
  one church united, strong and Spirit-filled;
  heirs to the fullness of your new creation
  in faith we follow, pledged to be your own;
  yours is the future, ours the celebration,
  for Christ is risen! God is on the throne!

4   **We travel on**

BUNESSAN   55 54 D

Words: Peter Atkins
Music: Gaelic melody

Gently

New age is dawn - ing, sun-rise is break - ing. Christ is re -

- veal - ing his way to us. Guard us and guide us, keep us and

feed us, we too would serve you, our Lord and God.

An arrangement with harmony by Martin Shaw can be found in *With One Voice*, No. 91 (Collins Liturgical Publications, London and Auckland, 1977), and in many other hymnbooks.

1 New age is dawning,
  sunrise is breaking.
  Christ is revealing
  his way to us.
  Guard us and guide us,
  keep us and feed us,
  we too would serve you,
  our Lord and God.

2 Yours is the true way
  for us to follow,
  finding a full life
  to share with all.
  Peace, hope and caring,
  joy, grace and loving,
  faith, trust restoring,
  your gifts in us.

3 Now to the future,
  God's new creation,
  our task to nurture,
  we travel on.
  War we will banish,
  children we'll cherish,
  the poor replenish,
  we'll take it on.

4 To God be glory,
  for Christ's love story,
  hope of the Spirit,
  touching us all.
  Our praises offering,
  our sins confessing,
  pardon receiving,
  God with us all.

Requests for permission to reproduce the words should be addressed to the author at 9A Paunui Street, Auckland 1005, New Zealand (Fax: 0064–9–5750477).

5 Lord of the years

LORD OF THE YEARS   11 10 11 10

Words: Timothy Dudley-Smith
Music: Michael Baughen

Lord, for the years your love has kept and guid- ed,
urged and in- spired us, cheered us on our way,
sought us and saved us, par-doned and pro- vid- ed:
Lord of the years, we bring our thanks to- day.

1 Lord, for the years your love has kept and guided,
   urged and inspired us, cheered us on our way,
   sought us and saved us, pardoned and provided:
   Lord of the years, we bring our thanks today.

2 Lord, for that word, the word of life which fires us,
   speaks to our hearts and sets our souls ablaze,
   teaches and trains, rebukes us and inspires us:
   Lord of the word, receive your people's praise.

3 Lord, for our land, in this our generation,
   spirits oppressed by pleasure, wealth and care:
   for young and old, for commonwealth and nation,
   Lord of our land, be pleased to hear our prayer.

4 Lord, for our world; when we disown and doubt you,
   loveless in strength, and comfortless in pain,
   hungry and helpless, lost indeed without you:
   Lord of the world, we pray that Christ may reign.

5 Lord, for ourselves; in living power remake us –
   self on the cross and Christ upon the throne,
   past put behind us, for the future take us:
   Lord of our lives, to live for Christ alone.

6

It all depends

Te Horo   97 97 97 87

Words and music: Colin Gibson

It all de-pends on where I'm go-ing if I reach my a-ny-where, but this I'm sure-ly, sure-ly know-ing, that I'll nev-er leave God's care. It all de-pends on when I'm travel-ling, may-be now or may-be then, but the Son of God will lead me through each

where and why and when. It all de - main.

1 It all depends on where I'm going if I reach my anywhere,
    but this I'm surely, surely knowing, that I'll never leave God's care.
    It all depends on when I'm travelling, maybe now or maybe then,
    but the Son of God will lead me through each where and why and when.

2 It all depends on how I'm choosing for the life that is in me,
    but I will never lose the hand of Christ, the one who walks with me.
    If I stumble or I falter he will steady me once more,
    for there is no darkest pathway that we cannot both explore.

3 It all depends on who comes with me if I break or if I bend,
    but this I'm surely, surely knowing, God will be there at the end –
    in the laughter and the sadness, in the pleasure or the pain,
    by my side and all about me God's own Spirit will remain.

Kindness – a children's song

Vivace ♩ = 112

Words and music: Colin Gibson

voices 1

voices 2

mf

Let me be kind to you, will you be kind to me? then we will live in a world where it is good to be, for we are held so ten-der-ly in God's big hands: here is a wink; **wink** here is a smile; **smile** here is a wave; **wave** here is my gift___ of **hands slowly outstretched,**

palms upwards

fine

kind - ness, here is my gift of lov-ing kind - ness.

Kind - ness,_____ Kind - ness, God shows us kind - ness, in the sun that lights the day, in the

Kind - ness,_____ friends with whom I play; kind - ness, such lov-ing kind - ness, when I

D.%. al fine

snug-gle down to sleep, all the blan-kets in a heap. Let me be

Let me be kind to you,
will you be kind to me?
then we will live in a world
where it is good to be,
for we are held so tenderly in God's big hands:
here is a wink; here is a smile; here is a wave;
here is my gift of kindness,
here is my gift of loving kindness.

1 Kindness, God shows us kindness,
    in the sun that lights the day,
    in the friends with whom I play;
    kindness, such loving kindness,
    when I snuggle down to sleep,
    all the blankets in a heap.

    Let me be kind to you . . .

2 Kindness, God shows us kindness,
    in the stories I am told
    by my granny who's so old;
    kindness, such loving kindness,
    through a world I may explore,
    always finding more and more.

    Let me be kind to you . . .

3 Kindness, God shows us kindness,
    in the apple on the tree,
    in the honey from the bee;
    kindness, such loving kindness,
    in the sparrow's cheerful song,
    in the place where I belong.

    Let me be kind to you . . .

4 Kindness, God shows us kindness
    through each baby girl and boy,
    in the life that I enjoy;
    kindness, such loving kindness,
    through God's very own dear Son,
    who loved each and every one.

    Let me be kind to you . . .

190

8   Where the love of God is guiding

RECONCILIATION   87 86 85 85

Words: Shirley Murray
Music: Jillian M. Bray

Where the love of God is— guid-ing there is now an-oth-er way:

new a-ware-ness of com-pas-sion learned from one an-oth-er;

love, the face of God in Je-sus, new cre-a-tion's thrust,

love, trans-form-ing tears and ter-ror in - to health and trust._____ be.

1   Where the love of God is guiding
    there is now another way:
    new awareness of compassion
    learned from one another;
    love, the face of God in Jesus,
    new creation's thrust,
    love, transforming tears and terror
    into health and trust.

2   Where the truth of God is driving
    there is now another way,
    shining through our times' confusion,
    sharp with revelation:
    words that stifle sense or spirit
    changed and redefined,
    crosses raised to teach division
    lowered, left behind.

3   Where the life on earth is dying,
    there is now another way,
    where the child may grow in safety,
    where there's peace and shelter,
    when we hold the fragile planet
    in our conscious care,
    when we see again as sacred
    all we are and share.

4   God will lead us on this mission,
    God, the flightpath and the power,
    lifting all who grasp the vision
    into understanding:
    so the heart and hope within us
    sets each other free,
    where the love of God is guiding,
    this shall come to be.

Requests for permission to reproduce the words and/or music should be addressed to Shirley Murray at PO Box 2011, Raumati 6450, Aotearoa/New Zealand.

Song for Epiphany

WINGATE WAY   10 10 10 10

Words: Shirley Murray
Music: Colin Gibson

Wise men came jour-ney-ing,
once long a-go,
ca-mel hooves swirl-ing the
sand dune and snow,___
gold___ in the sad-dle bag,
myrrh in the jar,
in-cense to ho-nour the Child of the star.

1 Wise men came journeying, once long ago,
   camel hooves swirling the sand dune and snow,
   gold in the saddle bag, myrrh in the jar,
   incense to honour the Child of the star.

2 Wise are the travellers led to move on,
   following the signs where the Christ light has shone,
   facing the deserts and crossing the lines,
   heeding no limits that culture defines.

3 Wise are each one of us looking for change,
   stargazer people, respecting the strange,
   inner and outer worlds open to light,
   centred on seeing the real and the right.

4 Wise ones keep journeying all through their days,
   bringing their gifts to the source of their praise,
   risking the Promise with all they hold dear,
   seeking God's peace at the door of the year.

From *Carol our Christmas* (New Zealand Hymn Trust).
Alternative music: BONNIE GEORGE CAMPBELL, published in *Every Day in Your Spirit* (Hope Publishing Company, Carol Stream, IL. 60188, USA).

10   God Weeps

COMPASSION   6 4 8 10

Words: Shirley Murray
Music: Peter Atkins

God weeps____ at love with - held, at strength mis -

- used, at child-ren's in - no-cence a - bused, and till we change the

way we love, God weeps. God waits.

1 God weeps
   at love withheld,
   at strength misused,
   at children's innocence abused,
   and till we change the way we love,
   God weeps.

2 God bleeds
   at anger's fist,
   at trust betrayed,
   at women battered and afraid,
   and till we change the way we win,
   God bleeds.

3 God cries
   at hungry mouths,
   at running sores,
   at creatures dying without cause,
   and till we change the way we care,
   God cries.

4 God waits
   for stones to melt,
   for peace to seed,
   for hearts to hold each other's need,
   and till we understand the Christ,
   God waits.

Alternative tune: HIROSHIMA, Carlton R. Young, 1996, USA.
From *Every Day in Your Spirit* (Hope Publishing Company, Carol Stream, IL. 60188, USA).

11

It's rising up

Words and music: Matt Redman
and Martin Smith

With expectation

It's ris - ing up___ from coast to coast, from

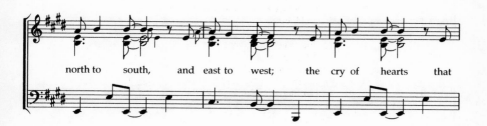

north to south, and east to west; the cry of hearts that

love your name, which with one voice we will pro - claim.___

___ 2. The

_ the earth. Oh, let the cry _ to na-tions ring, that

all may come and all may sing: Ho - ly

is _ the _ Lord. (Ev-ery heart sing:) Ho - ly

is _ the _ Lord. (With one voice sing:)

D.C. last time

(3. And)

198

1 It's rising up from coast to coast,
   from north to south, and east to west;
   the cry of hearts that love your name,
   which with one voice we will proclaim.

2 The former things have taken place,
   can this be the new day of praise?
   A heavenly song that comes to birth,
   and reaches out to all the earth.
   Oh, let the cry to nations ring,
   that all may come and all may sing:

   'Holy is the Lord.' (Every heart sing:)
   'Holy is the Lord.' (With one voice sing:)
   'Holy is the Lord.' (Every heart sing:)
   'Holy is the Lord.'

3 And we have heard the lion's roar,
   that speaks of heaven's love and power.
   Is this the time, is this the call
   that ushers in your kingdom rule?
   Oh, let the cry to nations ring,
   That all may come and all may sing:

   'Jesus is alive!' (Every heart sing:)
   'Jesus is alive!' (With one voice sing:)
   'Jesus is alive!' (All the earth sing:)
   'Jesus is alive!'

From *A Songs of Fellowship Worship Resource Music Book Two 1998*. Other suitable songs in that collection by Matt Redman are: No. 793, 'I dream of tongues of fire resting on your people'. No. 1106, 'We will give ourselves no rest till your kingdom comes on earth'. No. 1034, 'There is a louder shout to come, there is a sweeter song to hear'. No. 880, 'Let eveything that, everything that, everything that has breath, praise the Lord'.

Requests for permission to reproduce the words and/or music should be addressed to Kingsway's Thankyou Music, PO Box 75, Eastbourne, East Sussex BN23 6NW, England.

12

Come celebrate!

CLERKENWELL GREEN

Words and music: Michael Baughen
music arranged Gerard Brooks

With Vigour

Come ce-le-brate! Come and sing with praise! Come ce-le-brate! Hearts and voi-ces raise! Je-sus the King of_ kings.

Let all the na-tions bow to him, his rule is o-ver all. We bow_ the knee in a-dor-a-tion, Je-sus! Je-sus! He is Lord of_

1 Men: Come celebrate!   Trebles: *Come and sing with praise!*
  Men: Come celebrate!   Trebles: *Hearts and voices raise!*
  All: Jesus the King of kings.
       Let all the nations bow to him,
       his rule is over all.
       We bow the knee in adoration,
       Jesus! Jesus! He is Lord of all!

2 Men: Come celebrate!   Trebles: *In the earth and sky!*
  Men: Come celebrate!   Trebles: *Lift his name on high!*
  All: Jesus the Lord of lords.
       Through him the universe was made,
       he now sustains it all.
       He is the lord of all creation,
       Jesus! Jesus! He is Lord of all!

3 Men: Come celebrate!   Trebles: *In the world around!*
  Men: Come celebrate!   Trebles: *Let the trumpets sound!*
  All: Jesus the lamb of God.
       He is the saviour of the world,
       he died to save us all.
       His sacrifice brought us forgiveness,
       Jesus! Jesus! He is Lord of all!

4 All: Come celebrate!   All: *Al-le-lu-ia!*
  All: Come celebrate!   All: *Al-le-lu-ia!*
  All: Jesus the son of God.
       He shared our human frailty;
       he came to serve us all;
       now he is risen and exalted,
       Jesus! Jesus! He is Lord of all,
       he is Lord of all!

CONCLUSION

In this book I have endeavoured to set out the reasons why the year 2000 is a significant date for Christians to celebrate. I have told of the conviction we can bring to our witness at the beginning of a new millennium. I have set forth outlines for some public services that we might use as a basis for our celebrations. I have provided resources for 'Worship 2000' among congregations and in our personal times of prayer and reflection. I have shared the wisdom of Christian leaders and scholars from around the world. I have recorded the music which has been especially written for our new millennium singing. Only one more thing is needed to celebrate 'Worship 2000' with joy and enthusiasm – motivated Christians!

As I have discussed the topics in this book with individuals and groups in its time of preparation, I have heard of some hesitations from people who otherwise would want to be excited about the new millennium. Of course, they say, they would like to celebrate it, but they are held back by some concerns they have. As I draw this book to a conclusion I want to look at those concerns and show that there is a positive response to them.

First, I have found a fear of rejoicing in the face of the fact that the new millennium is bringing new burdens and troubles of its own making. There is the 'Millennium Bug' that may shut down many of the computers. Most computers have an automatically adjusted dating system, and the computer depends on accurate instructions from this system to carry out many of its other functions.[1] Therefore, if the programs have not been rewritten, the banking, communications, travel and security systems may fail to operate as the date changes, and a terrible chaos may result. Even if most computer programs can be rectified in time, the 'Millennium Bug' has been very costly in its consumption of human and financial resources, causing a slow-down in efforts to solve world economic and political issues. So how can Christians celebrate a significant date when the dating system itself is the cause of such terrible threats to the smooth operation of world societies?

The answer is surely that Christians have always celebrated God's presence and power in the midst of pain as well as pleasure. Year by year we celebrate Holy Week and Easter because we know that God does not desert us in the times of darkness. In the Eucharist we celebrate by remembrance the pain of the Cross as well as the new life of the Resurrection. Christians are experienced in celebrating even in the midst of uncertainty and confusion. Our celebrations for the year 2000 will be a powerful witness which gives hope to our world as it faces the future. As part of 'Worship 2000' we can use this prayer:

> In darkness and in light,
> in trouble and in joy,
> help us, gracious God,
> to trust your love,
> to serve your purpose,
> and to praise your name.

Secondly, there is concern that we are not being 'logical' in celebrating the year 2000. The argument is that this date was simply the result of human decisions to give prominence to the Christian Faith in the sixth century. Even then Dionysius Exiguus got it wrong and the birth of Jesus Christ took place earlier than the year '0'. So some Christians feel rather stupid and illogical in highlighting the year 2000 as a year in which Christians should celebrate a significant anniversary of the Incarnation. After all, it is not easy to celebrate while uttering a series of apologies!

Yet if we waited for a logical date on which to celebrate any event, we would find it hard to celebrate at all. With all the changes in the time zones around the world, it is difficult to say when an event really occurred in logical terms. I should probably celebrate my birth in Ireland on the day after my birthday, as I now live in New Zealand, where the clock is 12 hours ahead of GMT. The answer to this concern about a lack of logic over the date lies (as Professor Frances Young points out on pages 167–8) in seeing time as a sacrament, where 'remembrance' provides the significant links to reality. It is important to celebrate time events in that framework.

We can rejoice that past generations have given us this dating system in honour of the Incarnation of Christ and of the significance of that turning point in the history of humanity. In this context we can focus on remembrance in our worship and respond joyfully:

This is the day that the Lord has made:
Let us rejoice and be glad in it!

Thirdly, I have heard the concern expressed that Christians would show a lack of tolerance and sensitivity to their neighbours of other faiths or no faith by celebrating in public the date which has special Christian significance. It could be said that Christian imperial dominance has forced this dating system on an unwilling world. Such concerns about imperialism seem to lie behind the substitution of CE (meaning 'Common Era') for AD (meaning *Anno Domini,* 'in the year of our Lord'). Bishop Roger Herft has important points to make about religious groups feeling confident in their own celebrations (see pages 163–5).

I believe with him that Christians have every right to celebrate amidst a world community that does not all share the same religious beliefs. To celebrate does not show a lack of tolerance for others. Rather, not to celebrate shows a lack of conviction in the importance of the revelation of Jesus Christ, and as such is no contribution to the pilgrimage of discovery about the whole truth of God. If we have good news to share, then all religious people will want to hear it. Others will respect Christians for seeking the Spirit of God to make effective the message of peace and service to all, regardless of their race, gender or creed.

For many Christians there is a mounting excitement in their hearts as the opportunity to celebrate the year 2000 comes around. A millennium change is a once-only experience in a lifetime for everyone! It is worth getting excited. So they want to respond with *enthusiasm.* But can we dare let such an idea enter our mind? For some, enthusiasm is still politically incorrect and culturally embarrassing! Enthusiasm in general opinion belongs to slightly mad people who get carried away at worship or parties and go dancing like King David in the streets (2 Samuel 6:14). Other people with an English cultural heritage have deep in their psyche the words of Bishop Joseph Butler (1692–1752), who is reputed to have said: 'Enthusiasm is a horrid thing, a very horrid thing.'

Yet enthusiasm is part of every act of celebration and a key element in its fulfilment. We need the burst of enthusiasm to kick-start our energies for living. I learnt the joy of dancing as part of the act of worship while with a black African congregation in one of the parishes at Soweto. Exuberant joy needs to be shown through our bodies as well as our minds. Sport supporters and concert audiences both know how to celebrate what is excellent and good with their whole beings in an unreserved way.

My hope therefore is that 'Worship 2000' will give an opportunity for multitudes of Christians worldwide to celebrate a new millennium with the enthusiasm of head and heart. May we use this time as a sacrament to give thanks to God for the coming of Christ our Saviour, and to witness in word and action to a new way of living in a new millennium. Then the dreams of the young will have a chance of fulfilment. Then the world will become a global community showing responsibility and care for one another and for all God's Creation. All of this will give glory to God; the God who created time, space and place for all humanity to respond in adoration and enthusiastic praise.

Come, let the Holy Spirit inspire our celebrations with thanksgiving, joy and hope so that all may sing:

Now is the moment to affirm
Christ's rule of life and time,
Two thousand years have come and gone,
But still his vision calls us on
To service in Christ's name,
     To service in Christ's name.[2]

NOTES

INTRODUCTION

1. Kenneth Latourette, *A History of Christianity* (Eyre and Spottiswoode, London, no date given), p. 381.
2. Archbishop Desmond Tutu, *The Rainbow People of God* (Doubleday, London, 1994), p. 8.
3. Revelation 7:9.
4. Ephesians 4:12.
5. Micah 6:8.

CHAPTER 1

1. For a summary of texts and versions of the Bible see *The Collegeville Bible Commentary* (The Liturgical Press, Collegeville, Minnesota, 1989), pp. 17–24.

CHAPTER 2

1. See the relevant entries in F. A. Cross and E. A. Livingstone, *The Oxford Dictionary of the Christian Church*, 3rd edn (Oxford University Press, Oxford, 1997).
2. For commentaries on the Gospels of Luke and Matthew see C. F. Evans, *Saint Luke* (SCM Press, London, and Trinity Press International, Philadelphia, 1990); I. Howard Marshall, *The Gospel of Luke* (Paternoster Press, Exeter, 1978); Leon Morris, *The Gospel according to Matthew* (Eerdmans, Grand Rapids, 1992); David E. Garland, *Reading Matthew* (Crossroads Publishing Co., New York, 1993).
3. For the geography of the land, Foder's *Israel* (with an edition updated each year) provides a ready guide.

CHAPTER 3

1. *Polis* is the Greek word for 'city' and stands for a mutual corporate body of citizens.

CHAPTER 4

1. *Holy Bible, New Revised Standard Version* (Zondervan Bible Publishers, Grand Rapids, Michigan, 1990).
2. Words from a hymn arranged by Ueta Solomona of the University of the South Pacific in Fiji (1990).
3. Malcolm Muggeridge, *Something Beautiful for God* (Collins, London, 1971).
4. Ibid., pp. 74–5.
5. Ibid., p. 66.

CHAPTER 7

1. Kenneth Clark, *Civilisation* (BBC & John Murray, London, 1969), p. 17.
2. Ibid., p. 33.
3. Ecclesiasticus (Sirach) 44:1–15, adapted.
4. Dag Hammarskjöld, *Markings* (Faber and Faber, London, 1964), p. 36.
5. Adapted from Michel Quoist, *Prayers for Life* (Gill and Son, Dublin and Melbourne, 1963), pp. 55–7.
6. Music by Andrew Lloyd Webber, lyrics by Don Black and Charles Hart.
7. Malcolm Muggeridge, *Something Beautiful for God* (Collins, London, 1971), p. 69.
8. Ibid., p. 78.
9. Dag Hammarskjöld, op. cit., pp. 31–2. Changes for inclusive language are shown in italics.

CONCLUSION

1. In a computer system that uses only two numbers for the date, when '99' turns to the next year it records '00'. This causes confusion because the program has not been set for such a variant, which might indicate '1900' or '2000' or any other date ending in '00'. This may cause the computer to shut down all functions.
2. From Norman Brookes' hymn 'God of the Ages' (see p. 178).

INDEXES

GENERAL INDEX

INDEX OF SUBJECTS IN THE PRAYERS (CHAPTERS 7–9)

INDEX OF SUBJECTS IN THE MESSAGES FOR A NEW MILLENNIUM (CHAPTER 10)

INDEX OF THEMES IN THE HYMNS AND SONGS (CHAPTER 11)

Sub-themes